TRADITIONAL VE
TAPAS RECIPES
OF SPAIN

Malcolm Coxall

Cornelio
Books

Published by M.Coxall - Cornelio Books
Copyright 2014 Malcolm Coxall
First Published in United Kingdom, Spain, 2014
ISBN: 978-84-941783-4-4

Table of Contents

Preface

Why a book about vegetarian tapas?

As a life-long vegetarian and a devotee of Spanish traditional cuisine, it seemed only natural to create a cookery book that focuses on the many parts of Spain's traditional cuisine which do NOT contain meat or fish. Tapas are an important part of the Spanish culinary tradition and they have pretty much become universally popular, so a book of vegetarian tapas seemed a good way place to define just a few of the many examples of traditional meatless cooking from the Spanish countryside.

To the uninitiated it would seem that Spain is a meat eater's paradise but, in fact, this is a little deceptive. Despite the modern stereotypes of Spanish food, which centre on its use of Ibérico hams, fish dishes, wild-fowl, goat, lamb and rabbit in many of today's menus, the truth of the matter is that many traditional Spanish dishes are meatless for historical, economic and religious reasons.

For this reason I felt that it would be useful to the vegetarian diner to know what meatless tapas could be found in Spain, and useful for the chef wanting to preserve an important part of Spanish culinary tradition that are often forgotten in a world where new-found affluence often means "meat with everything".

A short history of food in Spain: In modern times, Spain is considered to be one of the powerhouses of European food production, but it was not always so. Spain has undergone long periods of acute food poverty and experienced many famines resulting from catastrophic harvest failures. Sometimes these failures were man-made, sometimes the result of adverse climatic conditions. The effect of these often violent historical fluctuations in food production and the ancient and colourful multi-cultural history of Spain have created an extremely interesting culinary diversity. The often difficult times in Spanish history have altered the way food is made, preserved and re-used to give rise to what we see today in modern Spain - one of the most distinctive, imaginative, healthy, delicious and least wasteful systems of cookery in Europe.

Why are there so many vegetarian dishes in Spain? The ability of the Spanish cook to improvise a miracle with limited materials is legendary. Many of the dishes for which the country is so famous now are, in fact, the result of improvisations using whatever materials are to hand. Paella is a classical example. There are literally an infinite number of recipes for this dish - dependent entirely on what is to hand in the kitchen at that moment. Thus, in hard times, when meat or fish were not readily available, many a classic Spanish dish was made entirely without either of them.

Influences on Spanish cuisine: In addition to frequent periods of food poverty, Spain was and is largely a rural country with most urban dwellers still having close connections with the land. This connection greatly alters the perspective of the people towards food, and the love of good, simple, local food is universal in Spain. As the saying goes, "the best olive oil is that from your own village".

Underlying many common Spanish recipes are religious practices. After the conquest of Spain by the Christians in the late 15th century until modern times, the population has been largely Catholic. This meant that the majority of the population felt obliged to conform to the many days of abstinence from meat - so-called holy days of obligation - including every Friday of the year. These religious observances were one source of inventiveness in Spanish cuisine - and the absence of meat was seen as a challenge to the cook to produce something equally nourishing and appetizing. Thus, virtually every traditional dish in Spain has some meatless alternative and it is not unusual to ask for something without meat in any restaurant in Spain. Indeed, as a vegetarian, it is quite refreshing that asking for a meatless dish in Spain hardly ever raises an eyebrow and, generally speaking, the chef will do his or her best to oblige. In many respects Spain is far ahead of its European neighbours with regards to meatless alternatives. In general the rule in a Spanish restaurant is "Ask and you shall receive".

One of the most profound influences on traditional Spanish food was the Moorish presence in Spain which lasted from the early 8th to the late 15th century. During this time new culinary techniques and ingredients poured into the country as the Arabs brought their favourite dishes, cooking methods, new herbs, spices, new food ingredients and efficiently irrigated agriculture into the kitchens and fields of "al-Andalus" from as far away as Arabia, India, Persia and East Africa. Indeed, it could be argued with some conviction that the very origins of the tapa derive from the concept of "mezze" - the popular Middle Eastern habit of serving numerous small and diverse dishes. "Mezze" is still a very popular way of serving food in many Arabic and North African countries and has its origins in India.

During several centuries in Spain's Moorish renaissance, cooking techniques and ingredients from India were mixed with almonds from

Syria, pomegranates from Persia, spices from China, the Far East and Africa and dozens of new and exotic vegetables from across the vast Arabic empires of the early Middle Ages. Moorish techniques still dominate the Spanish kitchen to this day, with their love of mixing sweet and savoury tastes and the frequent use of nuts, dried and fresh fruits to create interesting textures and tastes.

Finally, the last major change to Spanish cuisine happened with Columbus' discovery of the New World. The colonisation of America opened up another new wave of foods and tastes. Gradually, Spanish cooks and farmers adopted a whole range of exotic vegetables, fruits and spices into the own fields and kitchens and indeed some of the culinary traditions of native America were adapted by cooks back in the Spanish homeland. For example, some say that the humble tortilla, the so-called "Spanish omelette", started its career in the kitchens of the indigenous peoples of Central America. The tortilla is now the single most popular tapa dish in Spain. The discovery of America altered the Spanish cuisine profoundly.

Why traditional recipes? One of the purposes of this book was to identify and document traditional vegetarian tapa dishes and to help to preserve and spread these recipes. The modern popularity of tapas carries the risk of causing a decline in the diversity of the tapas being served. A casual stroll through many big Spanish cities will quickly reveal that a handful of well-known tapas tend to dominate the less adventurous tapas bars which have capitalised on the tourists' desire to eat tapas.

Gladly, this is not a universal trend and it is quite easy to escape this "tapas tourism" and find the real thing tucked down many a back street, generally well patronised by the local population rather than by the less critical tourist. Away from the big cities in the Spanish countryside, the diversity of the Spanish tapas really comes to life, with every village, province and region having its own local favourite dishes often based on local agricultural produce. Tapas creation is also a thriving culinary art, with every village chef constantly experimenting in inventing new tapas. It is truly an open art-form in food.

What is included? Generally speaking, the book includes recipes which are normally prepared without meat or fish. This means that the recipes are not simply "tapas minus the meat", but rather original tapa dishes which are not normally made with any meat or fish. We have included recipes using eggs and cheese for those vegetarians that eat eggs or cheese but as you will see, many of the recipes here use neither.

The recipes are exclusively Spanish with just a few exceptional tapas that have been adopted as Spanish over the centuries. The recipes use Spanish traditional preparation techniques although we have compromised on suggesting the use of a mechanised blender in some cases. The book includes everything from small, simple tapas to large complex appetisers and makes no distinction between rural and urban recipes. It contains hot and cold tapas, suitable for the snowy winters of Aragón as well as for the torrid summers of Andalucía.

What is not included? Some modern vegetarian recipes often use soy derivatives, such as tofu or other synthetic products as substitutes for meat. We do not include these, because they are simply not traditional Spanish ingredients and we are not searching for meat substitutes in this book. Rather we are documenting traditionally meatless tapas.

Also, there is a tendency amongst some cooks to adopt internationalised ingredients as tapas, such as "mini-pizzas" or sushi ingredients. This type of processed "mongrel" ingredient is neither Spanish nor a traditional tapa and we therefore exclude such concoctions in an effort to be completely authentic.

Conclusions: Despite the tendency in the rest of the world to homogenise and simplify our diets, Spain still offers a world of food diversity. The tapas tradition is a superb demonstration of this diversity with an almost limitless range of local recipes.

Here we present just a small cross-section of typical recipes, but without doubt there are many thousands more. We hope you enjoy these selected recipes; whether you prepare them yourself or have them as a tapa in your local bar.

---oOo---

1. Introduction

What is a Tapa?

A tapa is an aperitif snack which is almost always accompanied by a drink of some kind. Tapas can be hot or cold. They may be extremely simple or very complicated. They may be very tiny and delicate or quite substantial and hearty. Some tapas are based on a slice of bread, but many more are not. They can include soups, pickles, salads, stews, cheeses, pies, fricassees, sorbets and pâtés. Forget any preconceptions you may have about what comprises a tapa. There are no limits.

Tapas may be served at any time of the day with a drink but, in general, eating tapas is something that happens after work in the evening and is often a pre-dinner appetizer, so very often tapas are eaten between 19:00 and 22:00. In some bars in Spain, tapas have evolved into an entire, and quite sophisticated, cuisine. Customers can order many different tapas and combine them to make a full meal.

The primary meaning of "tapa" is cover or lid, but in Spain the word also became a term for this type of appetizer. The origin of the tapa is uncertain, but there are several theories which we will explore below.

Tapas have different names in different parts of Spain. They are sometimes referred to as pinchos (pintxos in the Basque language) in Asturias, in Navarra, in La Rioja, País Vasco, Cantabria and in some provinces, such as Salamanca, because many of them have a "pincho" or cocktail stick through them to hold the tapa together. In other parts of Spain the word montadito describes the local traditional tapas. A montadito is something "mounted", usually on a slice of bread.

Obviously, many tapas are made with meat or fish. However, there are at least as many which are entirely vegetarian and this large repertoire of vegetarian tapas is the subject of this book. Enjoy!

---oOo---

1.1 History of the tapa

There are many stories about how tapas came into existence and it is actually impossible to know exactly how the tradition began. There are some fairly unlikely explanations. The reality is that the practice of eating tapas probably came about because of the long time between lunch and dinner in the Spanish culinary timetable. In the heat of Spanish summers, dinner is often eaten late when the temperature has fallen to a more comfortable level. This can be quite late.

Despite this common-sense explanation, here we are going to explore some of the traditional explanations for the origin of the tapa.

The fruit fly theory: One commonly cited explanation for the tapa is that an item like a slice of bread or small plate would be placed on top of a drink to protect it from fruit flies. There is a widespread theory that at some point in the distant past it became a habit to top this "cover" with a little snack - a tapa.

Alfonso the Wise (el Sabio): One recurrent theory is that Alfonso the Wise in the 13th century started the tapas tradition when he was king of Castilla. He recovered from an illness by drinking wine with small dishes between meals. After regaining his health, the king ordered that taverns would not be allowed to serve wine to customers, unless it was accompanied by a small snack or "tapa". The idea was that it was healthier to eat something whilst drinking wine.

Strong cheese and cheap wine: A rather cynical theory tells us that tapas were invented as a marketing ploy sometime around the 16th century, when tavern owners from Castilla-La Mancha found out that the strong taste and smell of mature cheese could help disguise the smell of bad wine, thus "covering" it, so they started offering free cheese when serving cheap, low quality wine.

The rowdy sailor theory: One of the more plausible explanations surrounds King Felipe III, who in the 16th century passed a law in an effort to curb rowdy drunken behaviour, particularly among soldiers and sailors. The law stated that when one purchased a drink, the bartender was to place a cover or lid on the cup or glass, containing some small quantity of food as part of the purchase of the beverage. The intention was that the food would slow the effects of the alcohol, and fill the stomach to prevent the client from drinking too much.

The sand theory: One unlikely explanation says that King Alfonso XIII stopped at a tavern in the city of Cádiz in the early 1900s where he ordered a cup of wine. The waiter covered the glass with a slice of cured ham before offering it to the king, to protect the wine from the beach sand. (Cádiz is a very windy place.) The king, after drinking the wine and eating the tapa, ordered another wine "with the cover".

The Mediterranean traditions: Mezze and Antipasto: By far the most likely explanation for the existence of the tradition of eating small tapas in the evening originates in the basic reality that people in hot countries tend to eat dinner much later than in cooler Northern climates. Perhaps surprisingly, the highest temperatures in Spain occur around 5 or 6 pm, especially in towns and villages, where buildings are also radiating a lot of the heat that has accumulated during the day. It is not a pleasant time to eat and most people prefer to wait with dinner until the sun has set and it is more comfortable to enjoy a meal with family and friends in the relative freshness of the night. However, this does leave a very long gap without food from lunch at 2pm to dinner between 9pm and midnight. Hence in many Arab, Levantine and Mediterranean countries, various solutions have been found to assuage the hunger.

Antipasto: In Italy the antipasto (meaning "before the meal") is the appetizer served before dinner, often comprising many of the same types of dishes used in Spanish tapas. Generally antipasto is eaten at the table and is meant to be a gentle lead-in to a lengthy dinner.

Meze or mezze is a selection of small dishes served (sometimes to accompany alcoholic drinks) as appetizers before a main meal in the Near East and the Balkans. In the Levantine, Caucasian and Balkan cuisines mezze is served at the beginning of all large-scale meals. The word is found in all the cuisines of the former Ottoman Empire and comes from the Turkish word "meze" meaning "taste", "flavour", "snack", or "relish", borrowed from the Persian word "mazze" meaning "a taste or snack" or "mazīdan" meaning "to taste".

Mezze is still very popular in Greece, Cyprus, Iran, Iraq, Jordan, Turkey, Lebanon, Palestinian territories, Jordan and Syria, Romania, Bulgaria, Albania, Serbia, and Bosnia. The same dishes, served without alcoholic drinks, are called "muqabbilat" - meaning "starters" in Arabic.

Many of the dishes served as mezze are also common tapas in Spain and it seems likely that the mezze tradition came to Spain during the Moorish period, from the 8th to the 15th Century CE, in the same way that samosas were introduced to the Muslim Delhi Sultanate by chefs from the Middle East in the 10th century CE at around the same time. This era was one of Spain's great culinary renaissances.

---o0o---

1.2 The Tapas "Culture"

Officially, there is no "tapas culture" in Spain. Tapas are simply free snacks to go with a drink, served to guests in bars at the discretion of the bar owner. If you had travelled through Spain in the 1970s you would have found a tapas custom that was completely normal and unexceptional - you order a drink and you get a small tapa on the house. Depending on the region and the season, this might be something as simple as a piece of cheese or as complicated as a bowl of soup or stew.

The concept of charging for tapas was completely unknown in those days. Customers going to a bar or restaurant to eat would generally have a drink before their meal and a tapa was a simple appetizer to accompany the drink. You paid for the drinks and for your meal - not for the tapas.

Sometime in the late 1980s, several things happened in Spain. Firstly EU membership in 1986 brought more affluence to the people and opened up new parts of the interior of the country to tourism. This increased affluence (especially in the cities) also allowed for the vibrant bar and restaurant culture to emerge again after that long, dark period of Franco's fascist regime - a period when only a tiny elite had any kind of disposable income for such frivolities. Suddenly, people started to eat out more again and to socialise outside the home. Spain also collectively began to realise that it had a food culture that was not only excellent in quality but was in fact quite unique. The concept of tapas as a way of eating rather than just as a simple appetizer began.

It wasn't long before bar and restaurant owners saw the commercial opportunities in selling tapas and indeed of having "tapas bars" dedicated to enjoying this especially Spanish form of food. During the last decade the popularity of tapas has blossomed and has become an international phenomenon, with tapas bars opening in towns and cities across the world.

Meanwhile, back in Spain, urban tapas bars do a very healthy trade with tourists and locals alike. However, at the same time, the tradition of giving a free tapa has grown in popularity again, with bars actively trying to outdo their competitors in the generosity of the tapas they offer their clients. The economic crisis of the last few years has encouraged the re-emergence of free tapas, as restaurants and bars strive to capture market share in an environment where people have less to spend.

So, today, we arrive at a point where many bars offer both the traditional free tapa with each drink and also a menu of alternative tapas to buy. This seems to be the best of both worlds for the restaurateur, the customers and more importantly for the preservation and development of the ancient tradition of the tapa.

Tapas in other countries

Tapas also exist in some countries in Latin America, and such snacks are known as "bocas". In Mexico, similar dishes are called "botanas". In modern times, tapas have spread throughout the world and whilst many deviate significantly from their origins, the concept of eating several appetizers referred to as "tapas" is now extremely popular in the most unlikely places such as Japan, Australia and Russia.

A universe of tapas

There are many hundreds of tapas in existence and every region in Spain has its own. Many Spanish main-course dishes are served in small quantities as tapas. In fact, there are an infinite number of tapas because everyday, a chef or barman invents a new one somewhere in Spain.

Here we have assembled some of the more traditional meatless tapas that we know are popular in both urban and rural Spain, but our list is by no means exhaustive.

---oOo---

1.3 Traditional Ingredients and Techniques

1.3.1 Basic Ingredients:

Here is a list of the basic ingredients which you will need in order to prepare many of the recipes in this book. The list excludes fresh products.

Almonds - Keep some in the shell at all times. Shelled almonds tend to go soft, whereas almonds in the shell stay fresh for years. You can skin almonds (if necessary) by blanching them in boiling water for a few seconds.

Cheeses - You will need various types of cheese including the following:

- "Rulo de Cabra" (goats' cheese in a roll, used in many tapas dishes).

- Fresh goats' cheese - this is a white, feta-like cheese.

- A fresh creamy sheep cheese like Torta del Casar.

- A strong mature hard sheep cheese like Manchego Curado.

- A good cheese to gratinate - usually "Semi-Curado", made with blended cows', sheep and goats' milk. There are many of these.

- Requesón or "queso de Burgos".

- A cream cheese - either made from goats' or cows' milk. Usually with quite a neutral flavour and often mixed with herbs and garlic.

Cooking wines - Many dishes call for red or white wines; some require a sweet wine like Muscatel. Generally, for cooking it's not necessary to use the best wines. Nonetheless, the wine should be good. If it is palatable as a wine to drink, then it is also suitable for cooking.

Dried fruit - Raisins, dried figs, prunes, apricots and muscatel raisins are the most popular dried fruits used in Spain and crop up in many tapas dishes.

Dried herbs and spices - The main herbs and spices used in traditional Spanish dishes are: parsley, rosemary, thyme, oregano, chilli peppers, black and white pepper, sweet paprika powder, cinnamon powder, cumin, garden mint, fennel, saffron, and cloves.

Flour - When we refer to flour in these recipes we mean white, plain wheat flour, unless we specify otherwise. However, this does not mean that other flour types will not work and generally wholemeal flour is a healthier option.

Garlic - Many Spanish savoury dishes use garlic, often in quite large quantities. Don't skimp on it! Also keep some dried garlic and garlic powder handy. This is very useful if you suddenly discover you need to add more garlic late in the cooking.

Honey - Many Spanish recipes, including savoury recipes, use honey. No home in Spain would be without a couple of jars of honey. A good local general purpose honey is fine - organic is even better.

Miscellaneous ingredients include: baker's yeast, baking soda, plant-based food colouring.

Olives - Most recipes using olives in Spain will assume the use of green olives, but you can also add some black olives for variety - although black olives are not that popular in most of Spain (Aragón being an exception to this). Generally it is more convenient to use olives that are already stoned.

Olive Oil - You will probably need two types: one for cooking and one for dressing. Generally, people prefer a sweeter, fruitier olive oil for dressing and a more bitter olive oil for cooking. Experiment with several oils and then select a couple that suit your taste. Like wine, only you can really decide which olive oil suits your particular taste.

Pan Cateto - Many recipes call for bread and specify "pan cateto". Cateto is actually a traditionally baked, usually round loaf. It is readily available in any country baker's. Similar breads can be found in most rural communities in Spain.

Pasta - The generally used types are macaroni and flat pastas like tagliatelle or vermicelli, all of various sizes.

Rice - Many recipes call for the use of rice. We haven't specified which rice you should use, but in general in Spain, the most commonly used rice is round white rice (which is grown in Spain). However, all types of rice will work, but cooking times and conditions may need to be adjusted accordingly.

Stale bread - Never again throw yesterday's bread away. Many recipes use yesterday's hard bread to prepare a delicious dish today. Bread in Spain is best eaten fresh, because within a few hours the lovely fresh bread is usually rock-hard and so bakeries generally bake at least twice per day. But when the bread is hard it just gets used for a different purpose, so think ahead.

Sugar and syrup - Brown, white and Demerara sugar, caster sugar, molasses and golden sugar cane syrups are used in many sweet and savoury recipes.

Vinegar - Buy one basic white wine vinegar and one basic red wine vinegar and a cider vinegar. Vinegar is used in many recipes. Also buy some "vinagre de Jerez" for special purposes.

1.3.2 Traditional Cooking Techniques:

A sofrito: This is a warm sauce made from very finely chopped ingredients (that may vary according to the dish it will be added to), cooked in olive oil until soft. Usually it contains onions, tomatoes, garlic, parsley, paprika powder, salt, but the ingredients may vary slightly according to the precise recipe.

A majaillo (or majado, or mojado): This is made by grinding a number of ingredients together into a paste, usually with a mortar and pestle (or in a blender). This paste is then added to a dish during its preparation.

Use of herbs and spices: In many dishes involving pulses, the addition of spices like mustard, cumin and star anise are not just a matter of adding flavour or serving as a reminder of Spain's Arabic past, but also a good way to aid digestion - especially with some of the more heavy dishes.

1.3.3 Useful tools and utensils you will need: Apart from the usual kitchen tools and utensils you may find that you need the following to make these recipes:

- A blender with several speed settings. Handheld "stick" blenders are useful for small quantities.

- One small and one large mortar and pestle to make majaillo pastes which many recipes use.

- A purée mill. This is a hand-turned utensil for making purées like potato or tomato purée.

- An empanada mould. This is a simple tool that allows the chef to create perfectly shaped empanadas. The circular pastry is placed in the mould, filled with the chosen contents and then the mould folds in the middle and seals the edges of the empanada. These moulds are readily available and save a lot of messy work.

---oOo---

2. The Recipes

2.1 The Recipes - An Introduction

2.1.1 Notes about these recipes: Traditional recipes can be difficult to define very clearly because they tend to be less exact, less prescriptive, than modern recipes. Traditional cooks often work using a feeling for their ingredients which is somewhat above the need to weigh or measure all the ingredients exactly. Therefore, they often make assumptions about how a dish should be prepared. We have tried to eliminate this ambiguity as much as possible, but some trial and error is inevitable in any traditional cuisine.

For example, a good mature tomato in Spain often means that the tomato is extremely ripe and soft and has a high moisture content. In Northern Europe some cooks would not dream of using a very soft, over-ripe tomato, whereas in fact it is at that moment that a tomato is at its best. However, such large differences in moisture content can alter a recipe quite radically and we assume that the cook understands such concepts and how to tailor a recipe according to the materials available.

Optional ingredients: The flexibility within a traditional recipe means that some of these recipes refer to an ingredient or seasoning as "optional" or "to taste", meaning that you should add the ingredient at your own discretion. These can very often be quite big decisions for a cook to make, so it's worth thinking about these options in advance. Cooks in Spain tend to use less salt (in general) than is used in Northern European cuisine, but tastes vary, so obviously you should suit your personal preferences when deciding on the amount of various seasonings that you use. The same goes for garlic but generally speaking Spanish cuisine is very liberal about the amount of garlic used. Garlic is treated more as a vegetable ingredient than a seasoning.

Undefined number of servings: None of our recipes specify the number of "servings". One reason for this is that there are no rules about the size of a tapa serving. Therefore, you will sometimes need to judge for yourself how much of an ingredient you use for a particular number of servings. In Spain the size of a tapa can vary from a tiny mouthful to a very large hearty portion.

Local variants: Most recipes have very many local variants and these can be quite different from one district to another. We have tried to present the most popular variants for each tapa, but be aware that there are certainly many similar but different tapas with the same name, even within one province.

---oOo---

2.2 Tapas, Canapés and Montaditos with Bread and Toast

Many tapas are based on a slice of bread or toast, but there are many variants and language plays a part in distinguishing between the different types of bread-based tapas.

What is the difference between a tapa and a canapé?

So how is a canapé different from a tapa? Well, in fact it isn't different, except linguistically and socially. A canapé is a small quantity of food which is served as an aperitif or hors d'œuvre in exactly the same way as a tapa is served with a drink, usually preceding a meal. The only real difference is that a canapé sounds somewhat more refined than a tapa and canapés are served at organised parties or receptions. For the rest, the differences are an illusion. Tapas can be any kind of small dish served with any kind of drink at almost any time of day. The same is true of a canapé.

However, canapés do tend to be based on a small piece of bread or toast (as are many tapas), but tapas come in many forms, very often without bread, and as we have seen can be rice dishes, soups, salads etc. whereas canapés tend to be bite-sized appetizers.

What is a montadito?

For the Spanish, a montado is a flavourful topping on a small slice of baguette or other bread. Montados (or montaditos) are a quick and easy, common tapa throughout Spain.

Montaditos are widespread in Spain and have been a traditional dish since the fifteenth or sixteenth century and are believed to predate the sandwich. The root of the word "montadito" is in the Spanish verb montar ("to mount"), where small slices of bread are topped, or "mounted", with a variety of appetizing ingredients.

Having said this, montaditos can also be made without bread and we have given just a few examples where montaditos have a vegetable, bean or rice base. There are truly a limitless number of montaditos.

What is a tosta?

A walk through any Spanish grocery shop will reveal an amazing array of "tostas", small pieces of pre-toasted bread in all kinds of shapes, sizes and flavours. These pieces of toast are also prepared fresh to use

19

as a base for various tapa dishes. Toast is very popular in Spain and is either made by simply grilling bread or quite often by frying bread in a very hot pan with just a hint of olive oil. Generally speaking tostas are eaten with a generous splash of olive oil to soften the bread.

BRUSCHETTA CON TOMATE

Tomato Brochette

Ingredients:

Bread (slices of cateto bread or similar)
Cherry tomatoes
Garlic
Olive oil
Oregano or basil

Preparation:

1. Toast the bread and cut into small pieces for each tapa.

2. Cut the tomatoes into small pieces together with some garlic.

3. Dress the tomato mixture with salt and olive oil.

4. Spoon the mixture onto the toast and serve with a sprinkling of oregano or basil on top.

CANAPÉS PARA CÓCTEL

Cocktail Canapés

Ingredients:

> 1 courgette (not too thick)
> 1 onion
> 1 green pepper
> 1 tomato
> Cream cheese
> Salt
> Ground black pepper
> Olive oil

Preparation:

1. Wash and slice the courgette. Place the slices of courgette onto the grill and cook until almost ready to eat. Put aside - we will finish them off just before serving.

2. Chop the onion and pepper. Remove the pepper stalk and seeds. Fry the onion and pepper together in some olive oil.

3. Peel and chop the tomatoes and add these to the mix in the frying pan. Add salt and pepper to taste and sauté until everything is well cooked.

4. Return the courgette slices to the grill. When they are ready we can start to make the canapés.

5. Spread some cream cheese on each slice of courgette and add a little of the mixture of tomato, onion and green pepper.

6. Sprinkle with a favourite herb (basil or oregano, for example) and serve immediately.

CANAPÉS CON CREMA DE AGUACATE

Canapés with Creamed Avocado

Ingredients:

> 1 avocado (ripe)
> 1 quarter of a large onion
> Olive oil
> Salt
> Wholegrain bread toasted.

Preparation:

1. Blend the avocado with the onion until obtaining a creamy paste.

2. Add the salt and a little olive oil and blend the mix again briefly.

3. Spread the paste on small pieces of wholemeal toast and serve.

CANAPÉS DE ESPÁRRAGOS

Asparagus Canapé

Ingredients:

>4 slices of brown sandwich bread
>A handful of rocket leaves
>4 white asparagus, well drained
>1 red (bell) pepper or 1 sweet chilli pepper (piquillo)
>Mayonnaise with some basil, dill, coriander. to taste
>Capers
>Chopped walnuts
>Olives stuffed with red pepper
>4 cherry tomatoes
>Chopped chives

Preparation:

1. Blend together 1 or 2 tablespoons of mayonnaise, the pepper and 1 teaspoon of capers (well drained).

2. Spread the bread slices with this mixture and place some leaves of rocket on the mix.

3. Add one chopped asparagus per slice and decorate each slice with two halves of cherry tomato.

4. Sprinkle the canapé with chopped walnuts, olives and some chives.

CANAPÉS DE HIGOS Y QUESO

Sweet Fig and Cheese Canapé

Ingredients:

    Eight small bread rolls, halved lengthways and toasted
    2 large figs (or 4 small ones)
    Fresh goats' cheese
    2 teaspoons of sugar
    Honey

Preparation:

1. Put a piece of cheese in a bowl and blend in the sugar with a fork. Stir while continuing to crush the cheese until it becomes a smooth paste.

2. Wash the figs and split each into 4 quarters (or in 2 halves if the figs are small).

3. Spread each half of the toasted rolls with the cheese and add a piece of fig on top of the cheese. Finish off by drizzling some honey on top of each canapé.

CANAPÉS DE NUECES CON AROMA DE NARANJA

Orange-flavoured Walnut Canapés

Ingredients:

> 150 g of cream cheese
> 2 tablespoons of mayonnaise
> 1 orange
> 100 g of walnuts
> 8 slices of sandwich bread

Preparation:

1. Cut the slices of bread into four equal pieces. Put these in the oven for 5 minutes at 150°C, remove them from the oven and put them aside.

2. Blend the cheese with the mayonnaise, freshly squeezed orange juice, half the grated orange peel and the walnuts (keeping aside 1 nut for each canapé).

3. Once fully blended, spread the pieces of toast with the mixture, finish it off with a walnut and sprinkle with the other half of the grated orange peel.

CANAPÉS DE PASTA DE GUISANTES

Canapé of Pea Pâté

Ingredients:

>250 ml of fresh peas
>375 ml of rocket leaf
>60 ml of grated cheese
>1 teaspoon of grated lemon peel
>1 teaspoon of lemon juice
>1 clove of garlic
>1 baguette
>Mint leaves (1 per slice)
>Olive oil
>Salt

Preparation:

1. Cook the peas in salted water until tender (about 8 minutes). Drain, and put them into a bowl of iced water so as to stop them cooking and to keep their colour.

2. Drain and put the peas into a blender with 60 ml of olive oil, the rocket leaves, the cheese, lemon juice and peel, and a little salt and pepper to taste.

3. Blend the mix into a light paste. Let it cool completely and put it into the fridge.

4. Meanwhile, cut the baguette into slices and put these into a preheated oven at 200°C to toast them. When ready, take the bread out, rub each slice with garlic and add a drop of olive oil and a mint leaf to each slice.

5. Finally, spread each slice with the pea pâté and serve.

CANAPÉS DE PÂTÉ DE ACEITUNAS NEGRAS

Canapés with Black Olive Pâté

Ingredients:

> Black olive pâté (see recipe under Pâtés)
> Small tostada biscuits (biscottes) or homemade tostadas
> Tomato in slices
> Sesame seeds

Preparation:

1. Spread the biscottes with some olive pâté and place a slice of tomato on top.

2. Sprinkle some sesame seeds on the canapés and serve.

CANAPÉS DE PIQUILLO

Pepper Canapé

The piquillo pepper is a variety of small sweet pepper (capsicum) that is traditionally grown in Northern Spain near the town of Lodosa. Its name is derived from the Spanish meaning a "little beak". The peppers are hand picked when red, during two harvests between September and December. They are then roasted, which gives them a distinct sweet, spicy flavour. They are then peeled and de-seeded by hand, before being packed into jars or tins for sale. Piquillo peppers are often stuffed with various fillings and served as tapas.

Ingredients:

> 8 piquillo peppers
> 8 small slices of bread
> Breadcrumbs
> 1 egg
> 1/2 red sweet pepper
> 1/2 green pepper
> 1/4 onion
> Olive oil for frying
> Salt

Preparation:

1. To make the stuffing: Chop the onions and peppers and fry with some salt (to taste) in a little olive oil. When they are soft, drain to remove the oil and let them cool.

2. Next, fill the piquillo peppers with the cold mix and put aside.

3. When the peppers are all filled, dip them in beaten egg and then coat them with breadcrumbs.

4. Fry the stuffed peppers in hot oil until golden brown.

5. When ready, remove and place them on absorbent kitchen roll.

6. Finally, place each pepper on a slice of bread and serve hot.

CANAPÉS DE QUESO DE CABRA CON ACEITE DE AJO

Goats' Cheese Canapé with Garlic Dressing

Ingredients:

>Sliced round bread (not too thick or too large)
>A roll of goats' cheese (Rulo de Cabra)
>Garlic oil (Ref. the note below - Olive oil and garlic)

Preparation:

1. Toast the bread in the oven until golden and crisp.

2. Cut the cheese into slices of 0.5 cm thick. This is easier if the cheese is put in the freezer first to cool and using a knife that has been immersed in hot water. Place each slice of cheese on a slice of bread.

3. Pour a little garlic oil over each canapé and place them under a grill until the cheese is melted.

Note: To make the garlic oil, put some olive oil (250 cc) in a sterilised glass bottle with 5-10 cloves of garlic, peeled and thoroughly washed, together with some black peppercorns and a slice of lemon. Seal the bottle and store in the refrigerator for a week before use. It is **extremely** important to refrigerate the oil and to use the slice of lemon, because the citric acid in the lemon inhibits anaerobic bacterial growth in the garlic. After it is aromatised, use up all of the oil immediately. You must not keep the garlic oil for later use.

CANAPÉS DE QUESO Y ACEITUNAS

Cheese and Olive Canapé

Ingredients:

    100 g of olives
    2 tablespoons of pine kernels
    150 g of cheese (use any cheese but cream cheese or manchego are suggested)
    3 tablespoons of olive oil
    1 clove of garlic
    Olives for garnish
    Bread for the canapés

Preparation:

1. Make sure the olives are stoned. Peel and finely chop the garlic.

2. Blend the olives, garlic, pine kernels and olive oil together into a fine paste.

3. Spread the slices of bread with the olive paste and add a piece of cheese. Finally, decorate each canapé with half an olive and serve.

CANAPÉS DE QUESO BLANCO

Fresh Cheese Canapé

Ingredients:

> 1 baguette
> 1 or 2 tomatoes
> Fresh cheese (Queso blanco)
> Fresh parsley
> 2 cloves of garlic
> Olive oil
> Salt

Preparation:

1. Quickly blanch and peel the tomatoes. Chop the tomatoes into small cubes and remove the seeds.

2. Make a machado: Peel the garlic and grind it in a mortar with a little salt, a dash of olive oil and some fresh, chopped parsley. Crush this well into a paste.

3. Slice the bread (the slices can be toasted if you prefer), spread each slice with a little of the machado and place some fresh cheese on each slice.

4. Finally place some tomato on top of the cheese. Serve immediately to ensure that the bread (or toast) remains dry and crisp.

CANAPÉS DE QUESO, HIGO Y CILANTRO

Cheese and Fig Canapé

This is a variant on the previous cheese and fig canapé, using coriander.

Ingredients:

> 1 baguette
> Fresh goats' cheese
> 6 or 7 figs
> Fresh coriander leaf

Preparation:

1. Slice the baguette diagonally.

2. Put a piece of cheese on each slice of bread, large enough to cover it.

3. Wash and dry the figs, cut them into slices and place one on top of the cheese.

4. Add a little honey and season with 1 or 2 coriander leaves.

CANAPÉS DE REMOLACHA Y QUESO

Beetroot and Cheese Canapé

Ingredients:

> 500 g of beetroot
> 1 baguette
> Olive oil
> Freshly ground pepper
> Cream cheese
> Chives
> Salt

Preparation:

1. Put the whole beetroot in a bowl; add a little water and cover the bowl with aluminium foil. Place in a hot oven for about an hour until soft. Then remove from the oven and allow to cool completely.

2. Peel the beetroot and cut it into slices. Stir in a little olive oil and some salt and pepper. Mix well.

3. Slice the bread and spread a little olive oil on each slice. Place the slices in a hot oven and let them bake until golden brown.

4. When the bread is ready, place a piece of beetroot on each slice. Then add some cream cheese on top of the beetroot.

5. Garnish with chopped chives and serve.

CANAPÉS DE TOMATE

Tomato Canapé

Ingredients:

>1 loaf of bread (like a baguette)
>4 tomatoes
>Olive oil
>Balsamic vinegar

For the pesto:

>50 g of basil leaves
>3 cloves of garlic
>4 tablespoons of pine kernels
>125 ml of olive oil
>100 g of grated cheese
>Pepper
>Salt

Preparation:

1. Make a pesto using a blender: Blend the basil, peeled garlic and pine kernels together. Add a little olive oil, blend again and then gradually add the remaining olive oil, stirring all the while. Finally, add the cheese and a little salt and pepper. Give the pesto a final touch with the blender.

2. Slice the bread and put the slices onto a tray and place this into a preheated oven at 200ºC. Let the bread toast until golden.

3. Meanwhile, cut the tomatoes into very small pieces. Also prepare a dressing by mixing a generous amount of olive oil with a little balsamic vinegar to your taste. Put aside.

4. When the bread is toasted, remove from the oven and spoon a little pesto on each slice; then place some of the chopped tomato on top of the pesto.

5. Finally, pour a little of the olive oil and vinegar dressing on each canapé and serve.

CANAPÉS DE TOMATE Y QUESO

Cheese and Tomato Canapé

This is a simple and tasty canapé, which is fast and easy to prepare.

Ingredients:

> Slices of bread
> Creamed cheese (preferably a strong cheese)
> 2 or 3 tomatoes
> Basil leaves

Preparation:

1. Dice the tomatoes.

2. Toast the bread.

3. When the bread is toasted, spread it with cheese and add a few pieces of tomato and, finally add some basil leaves. Cut to canapé size and serve immediately when the toast is still crispy.

HUEVOS DE CODORNIZ CON PISTO

Quails' Eggs on Toast with Pisto

Ingredients:

    Quails' eggs (1 per slice of bread)
    Baguette
    Tomato pisto (see recipes under Pisto)
    Olive oil

Preparation:

1. Cut the bread into thin slices, toast these and place them in a flat dish.

2. Heat the pisto and spread a spoonful on each slice of bread.

3. Fry the quails' eggs in plenty of oil and place one egg on each slice of bread.

4. Season with salt and pepper and serve.

MIGAS DE HARINA O CORTIJERAS DE MÁLAGA

Crumbs of Semolina of Málaga

This is a traditional "migas" dish from the province of Málaga. It uses semolina flour instead of breadcrumbs.

Ingredients:

> 0.5 kg of semolina flour
> 1 litre of water
> 1 head of garlic
> 0.5 litre of olive oil
> Salt (to taste)

Preparation:

1. First chop and stir-fry the head of garlic.

2. Add the water and some salt.

3. Bring this to the boil and begin to mix in the flour gradually whilst stirring, until the mix has the consistency of porridge.

4. Stop adding the flour, but continue stirring until the mix starts to form loose, fluffy crumbs.

5. Leave them to toast in the pan for a while until the consistency is just right.

6. Serve hot with a garnish of your choice.

MIGAS CASTELLANAS O DE PASTOR

Breadcrumbs of Castilla or Shepherd's Breadcrumbs

Ingredients:

> White bread (hard)
> Water
> 2 teaspoons of paprika (sweet, hot or mixed, according to taste)
> Oregano (to taste)
> Garlic
> Salt
> Olive oil

Preparation:

1. Chop the bread into small pieces (1 or 2 cm maximum). This takes a long time by hand so best to use a blender. Be careful not to mince it for too long, otherwise the bread is unusable. Put the pieces in a large bowl that allows you to stir them.

2. Warm up a couple of centimetres of water in a saucepan (don't let it boil) and add a little salt, the paprika and oregano. When thoroughly mixed let the water cool. Then slowly add the water to the breadcrumbs, being careful not to soak them too much. Add a splash of water and mix this in. As you progress, check the taste and, if necessary, add more salt, paprika and oregano to your taste. When all the breadcrumbs are moist, cover the bowl with a cloth and let it stand overnight.

3. Fry several cloves of garlic in olive oil. Add the breadcrumbs and fry the mix on a medium heat, stirring and breaking up any large pieces. When the crumbs are dried and turning brown, they are ready to serve.

Migas can be served alone or with eggs, fruit or vegetables of your choice.

MONTADITOS DE AGUACATE

Montadito with Avocado

This is a very simple montadito, and very easy to prepare:

Ingredients:

> 1 ripe avocado
> A slice of baguette or similar
> The juice of half a lime
> Salt
> Black pepper
> Fresh parsley

Preparation:

1. Scoop out the flesh of the avocado and put it in a bowl.

2. Add the juice of half a lime and some salt and pepper to taste.

3. Crush and mix everything with a fork until obtaining a smooth paste.

4. Spread this mixture on the slices of bread.

5. Serve with a topping of freshly chopped parsley.

MONTADITO DE BERENJENA, TOMATE Y QUESO

Montadito of Aubergine, Tomato and Cheese

There are many versions of this montadito based on aubergine. You can use a variety of vegetables such as courgettes or peppers etc. and you can make multiple layers of vegetables mixed with cheese. You can also season with several different herbs such as basil or parsley. This is a montadito with which to experiment.

Ingredients:

> 1 large aubergine
> 3 large tomatoes
> Slices of tetilla cheese
> 2 cloves of garlic
> Olive oil
> Coarse salt
> Fennel, chopped

Preparation:

1. Wash and cut the aubergine into slices with a thickness of about 0.5 cm. Sprinkle them with salt and leave them to stand for 30 minutes.

2. Meanwhile, wash and cut the tomatoes into slices and arrange them on a plate. Add a little oil and salt, and set aside.

3. Dry the aubergine slices with a paper towel.

4. Fry the chopped garlic in a little olive oil. When the garlic begins to brown, add the aubergine slices and sauté them for about 3 minutes per side.

5. When the aubergines are browned, place them on a plate, one beside the other.

6. Put a slice of tomato on each slice of aubergine, and add a slice of cheese. Bake in a pre-heated oven at 180ºC for about 15 minutes or until the cheese melts.

7. Season with a little coarse salt and olive oil and sprinkle with the chopped fennel.

8. Serve hot, optionally on a piece of toasted bread.

MONTADITOS DE CHAMPIÑONES

Montadito of Garlic Mushrooms

Ingredients:

>Sliced baguette
>250 g of mushrooms
>1 large onion
>1 clove of garlic
>Olive oil
>Black pepper
>Fresh parsley

Preparation:

1. Fry the onions gently in olive oil. Add the sliced mushrooms and sauté.

2. When the mushrooms are nearly tender, add the crushed garlic, freshly chopped parsley and a little black pepper.

3. When the mushrooms are cooked, put a tablespoonful of the mix onto each slice of baguette and serve hot.

MONTADITO DE CHAMPIÑONES CON PIMIENTOS

Montadito of Mushrooms and Peppers

Ingredients:

> 500 g of mushrooms, coarsely chopped
> 3 red peppers, roasted, peeled and cut into strips
> 2 cloves of garlic, finely chopped
> 4 tablespoons of olive oil
> Salt to taste
> Slices of baguette

Preparation:

1. Stir-fry the mushrooms in hot olive oil until they are golden brown (about 4 minutes).

2. Reduce the heat to medium and add the strips of red pepper and the chopped garlic. Mix the ingredients together well.

3. Add salt to taste and cook until the mushrooms are cooked and the garlic is golden brown.

4. Put a slice of baguette on a small plate and cover it with 1 or 2 tablespoons of the mushroom and pepper mixture.

5. Serve hot.

MONTADITOS DE CHAMPIÑONES Y QUESO DE TORTA DEL CASAR

Montadito of Mushrooms and Torta de Casar Cheese

Ingredients

Pre-cooked mushrooms (sliced and parboiled or from a jar)
A slice of baguette cut lengthways, or other crusty bread
1 onion (cut into small cubes)
Torta del Casar cheese
Salt
Olive oil
Garlic (minced)
Fresh parsley

Preparation:

1. Marinate a little fresh parsley in some olive oil overnight.

2. Sauté the pre-cooked mushrooms with the onion, the garlic and the rest of the parsley in a little olive oil. Add salt to taste. When the onions are brown, take the pan off the heat.

3. Pour the mixture over the bread. Spoon on some of the Torta del Casar cheese. Place under a hot grill until the cheese begins to toast.

4. Serve hot with some of the parsley and olive oil marinade on top.

MONTADITO CON CONFITURA DE HIGOS Y QUESO ARZÚA-ULLOA

Montadito of Arzúa-Ulloa Cheese with Fig Jam

Here is an example of a tapa using the creamy Galician cheese called Arzúa-Ulloa in combination with sweet fig jam and nuts. It makes a delicious taste combination.

Ingredients:

For the fig jam:

1 kg of ripe figs
500 g of sugar
100 ml of water
Juice of 1 lemon
Half a teaspoon of cinnamon
1 clove

For the montadito:

Slices of cateto bread or similar country bread
120 g of Arzúa-Ulloa cheese
50 g of walnuts
A few sprigs of fresh parsley
Olive oil

Preparation:

For the fig jam:

1. Wash the figs and cut them into quarters. Put them in a bowl and sprinkle them with the lemon juice. Leave aside.

2. Add the sugar to 100 ml of water in a saucepan and bring to the boil. When all the sugar is dissolved, add the figs and let the mix simmer for about 15 minutes, stirring occasionally. Take the pan from the heat and put aside until the jam cools and thickens.

For the montadito:

1. Toast the slices of bread. Pour a little olive oil over each one.

2. Cut the cheese into portions and place one on each slice of bread.

3. Spoon a portion of fig jam on the cheese. Serve the montaditos decorated with a walnut and a few leaves of fresh parsley.

MONTADITO DE ESPÁRRAGOS VERDES Y MOSTAZA

Montadito of Green Asparagus and Mustard

Ingredients:

> 1 slice of bread
> 1 boiled egg yolk
> Half a tablespoon of lemon juice
> 3 thick green asparagus tips
> Half a tablespoon of coarse mustard
> 2 tablespoons of olive oil
> Ground black pepper
> Fine salt
> Coarse salt

Preparation:

1. Toast a slice of bread.

2. Blend the boiled egg yolk with the mustard, the lemon juice, oil, pepper and fine salt.

3. Grill the asparagus tips with a little olive oil until tender.

4. Spread the mustard mix on the toasted bread and place the asparagus tips on top with a pinch of coarse salt.

5. Serve warm.

MONTADITO DE ESPÁRRAGOS Y QUESO MANCHEGO

Montadito of Asparagus and Cheese of La Mancha

The combination of asparagus and manchego cheese is very good because the salty manchego cheese enhances the flavour of the asparagus.

Ingredients:

> 40 green asparagus tips
> 100 g of manchego cheese
> 1 baguette
> 250 g of ripe tomatoes
> Olive oil
> Salt

Preparation:

1. Put the asparagus tips in a saucepan with boiling water and cook them for just one minute. Then drain them and put them in cold water to stop the boiling.

2. Cut 8 slices of bread (about 2 centimetres thick).

3. Cut the tomatoes open and rub them into the bread. Add a splash of oil and a pinch of salt.

4. Quickly sauté the drained asparagus tips in a frying pan with a tablespoon of olive oil, until they are hot and lightly browned.

5. Use a peeler to cut some thin slices of manchego cheese.

6. Put the bread on a plate, place 5 asparagus tips on each and cover these with slices of manchego cheese.

7. Serve warm.

MONTADITO DE GRANADA Y QUESO DE CABRA

Montadito of Goats' Cheese and Pomegranate

The fruit of the pomegranate combines very well with cheese, especially with creamy goats' cheese, and makes an unusual and healthy montadito.

Ingredients:

> 200 g of goats' cheese ("rulo de cabra")
> 1 ripe pomegranate
> 1 mandarin orange
> 1 apple
> 1 baguette (cut into slices)
> 0.5 l of vinegar of Jerez

Preparation:

1. Reduce the vinegar in a small pan with two tablespoons of sugar. Let it boil until it takes on a denser consistency.

2. Meanwhile, split the pomegranate in half, turn it upside down over a bowl and tap with a spoon to collect all seeds. Peel and cut the apple into small cubes. Coat the apple with a little lemon juice to prevent it from going brown. Peel the mandarin orange and divide it into slices. Mix all the fruit together in a bowl. Add the reduced vinegar when it is ready and mix well.

3. Cut the roll of goats' cheese into slices with a thickness of about 2 cm. Fry these in a very hot frying pan to toast the outside, creating a crust, but leaving the inside tender and soft.

4. When the cheese is toasted, simply place a piece of cheese on each slice of bread.

5. Add a topping of the fruit and serve immediately.

MONTADITO DE HUEVOS DE CODORNIZ, FREJOLES Y ARROZ

Montadito of Quails' Eggs, Canary Beans and Rice

Ingredients:

> 280 ml of cooked "Canary beans"
> 210 ml of cooked white rice
> 1 tablespoon of olive oil
> 5 tablespoons of chopped onion
> 2 cloves of garlic
> 6 quails' eggs, fried
> Coriander leaves

Preparation:

1. Mix the beans with the rice in a bowl.

2. Heat the olive oil in a frying pan and sauté the onion and garlic for four minutes.

3. Add the mixed beans and rice to the pan and fry the mixture together, turning it over for about four minutes until a crust forms. In a separate frying pan, fry the quails' eggs until cooked.

4. Serve small portions of beans and rice on individual plates with a fried quails' egg on top. Garnish with some chopped coriander leaves.

MONTADITO DE PATÉ DE ACEITUNAS Y HIGOS
Montadito of Olive and Fig Tapenade

Ingredients:

> 200 g of chopped dried figs
> 125 ml of water
> 1 tablespoon of olive oil
> 2 tablespoons of wine vinegar
> Large pinch of chopped fresh rosemary
> Large pinch of chopped fresh thyme
> 0.25 teaspoon of cayenne pepper
> 150 g of stoned green or black olives, chopped
> 3 cloves of garlic, crushed
> Salt
> Freshly ground black pepper
> 5 tablespoons of chopped roasted walnuts
> 200 g of fresh goats' cheese
> 1 baguette

Preparation:

1. Mix the figs with the water in a saucepan over medium heat. Bring to the boil and cook until tender and the liquid has reduced. Remove from the heat and stir in the olive oil, vinegar, rosemary, thyme and cayenne.

2. Add the chopped olives and garlic and mix well. If you prefer a smoother, creamier pâté you can use a blender.

3. Season with salt and pepper. Cover and refrigerate for 4 hours or overnight to allow to marinate.

4. Cut a baguette or similar bread into slices and toast it on both sides. Spread the cheese on the toasted bread and spoon the tapenade over the cheese.

5. Sprinkle with the chopped roasted walnuts and serve.

MONTADITOS DE PIMIENTOS Y ALCACHOFA

Montaditos of Artichoke and Roasted Pepper

This is a simple montadito tapa recipe made with roasted red peppers and artichoke hearts. You can prepare these ingredients from fresh materials or buy them ready cooked and use them directly in the recipe.

Ingredients:

> 1 baguette
> 350 g of roasted red peppers
> 500 g of cooked artichoke hearts
> 2 cloves of garlic
> Olive oil
> Red wine vinegar

Preparation:

1. Slice the baguette. Toast the slices on both sides. Set aside for later.

2. Drain the liquid from the red peppers and the artichoke hearts; put them into a blender and coarsely chop the peppers and artichokes. Place the mix in a bowl.

3. Peel and mince the garlic, add it to the pepper mixture and mix by hand.

4. Pour a little olive oil and vinegar over the mixture. Mix thoroughly.

5. Spoon the mixture onto the toasted slices of baguette just before serving.

MONTADITO DE PERAS CARAMELIZADAS CON QUESO DE CABRA Y ALMENDRAS

Montadito of Caramelised Pears with Goats' Cheese and Almonds

---

Ingredients:

> 2 slices of crusty bread
> A teaspoon of butter
> 1 pear, peeled and diced
> 1 teaspoon of vinegar
> 1 tablespoon of honey
> Salt and pepper
> 1 slice of goats' cheese (rulo de cabra) broken into pieces
> Roasted almonds, coarsely chopped

Preparation:

1. Sauté the pear in butter, add honey and vinegar and cook until caramelized. Add a little salt and pepper.

2. Toast the slices of bread.

3. Spread the slices with some cheese and add the hot caramelised pears. Sprinkle with chopped almonds. Serve hot.

MONTADITOS DE PIMIENTOS CON QUESO CREMA

Montadito of Peppers with Cream Cheese

Ingredients:

3 small peppers
3 tablespoons of cream cheese (or fresh goats' cheese)
1 tablespoon of milk
Fresh basil
Fresh parsley
Salt
Pepper
A quarter of an onion
1 baguette
2 cloves of garlic

Preparation

1. Mix the cream cheese with the milk to form a smooth cream.

2. Finely chop the basil, garlic and the onion and mix these into the cheese. Season the cheese with salt and pepper. Keep a few basil leaves for decoration.

3. Cut the tops of the peppers and remove the seeds.

4. Fill the peppers with the cheese mix.

5. Preheat the oven to 100°C. Place the peppers upright in the oven for at least 30 minutes. They should be warm, but not cooked.

6. Remove the peppers from the oven and cut each one in half. Place the segments onto slices of baguette already spread with some fresh cheese.

7. Garnish with basil leaves or a little chopped parsley and serve.

MONTADITOS DE PISTO

Montadito with Pisto Stew

Ingredients:

    4 tablespoons of olive oil
    2 large aubergines
    2 red peppers
    1 large ripe tomato
    2 cloves of garlic
    Grated zest and juice of 1/2 lemon
    1 tablespoon of chopped fresh coriander and a few sprigs for garnish
    1 teaspoon of paprika powder
    Slices of fresh bread or toast
    Salt
    Black pepper

Preparation:

1. Preheat the oven to 190°C.

2. Pierce the skin of the aubergine and the peppers and coat them with 1 tablespoon of olive oil. Place them in an ovenproof dish to roast in the oven for 45 minutes or until the skins begin to blacken, the flesh of the aubergine is tender and the peppers are cooked.

3. Place the roasted vegetables in a bowl and cover. Let them stand for 15 minutes, until they have cooled down.

4. Cut the aubergines in half lengthwise, scoop out the flesh and throw away the skin. Cut the flesh into large chunks. Cut the stem off the peppers, de-seed them and cut them into thick slices. Cut up the tomato into small pieces.

5. Fry the tomato for about 5 minutes than add the aubergine and pepper and fry for about 5 minutes more in the remaining olive oil. Then add the minced garlic and fry for around 30 seconds. Add the lemon zest and lemon juice, coriander, paprika powder, salt and pepper.

7. Serve warm, at room temperature or cool for 30 minutes, then refrigerate for 1 hour if you prefer to serve the montadito cold.

8. Spoon the pisto onto slices of fresh or toasted bread. Optionally, you can garnish with some freshly chopped coriander.

MONTADITO DE QUESO CREMA Y PIQUILLOS

Montadito of Cream Cheese with Red Peppers of Lodosa

Ingredients:

> 190 g of cream cheese
> 130 g of piquillo red peppers (Lodosa), chopped
> 130 g of tomato, chopped
> 6 chopped green olives
> 4 tablespoons of olive oil
> Salt to taste
> Pepper to taste
> 6 slices of baguette
> 6 parsley leaves

Preparation:

1. Spread cream cheese on each slice of bread.

2. Mix together the chopped red peppers, chopped tomatoes, chopped olives and olive oil. Add salt and pepper to taste.

3. Put a tablespoon of this mixture on top of the cheese on each slice of baguette.

4. Decorate with a leaf of parsley and serve.

MONTADITO DE QUESO IDIAZÁBAL Y CEBOLLA
Montadito Idiazábal Cheese and Onion

Idiazábal is a hard, matured cheese made from un-pasteurised sheep milk, usually from Latxa and Carranzana sheep of the towns of Urbia, Entzia, Gorbea, Orduña, Urbasa and Aralar in the País Vasco and Navarra. It has a somewhat smoky flavour, although it is usually not smoked. Idiazábal has been granted protection under the system of Denominación de Origin (D.O.) of Spain and the E.U. It has a nutty, buttery flavour and is eaten fresh, often with quince jelly or other sweets.

Ingredients:

> Slices of bread (baguette or similar crusty bread)
> A slice of cheese for each slice of bread
> 1 onion
> Peppercorns
> Olive oil
> A little honey
> A glass of milk

Preparation:

1. Cut the cheese into slices and allow it to warm to room temperature.

2. Peel and cut the onion into very thin strips and put them to soak in a bowl with the milk and peppercorns for 30 minutes. After soaking the onions place them onto kitchen paper to dry.

3. Fry the onions in olive oil until crisp, remove them from the pan and let them drain on kitchen paper.

4. In the meantime, toast the bread and whilst it is still hot put a slice of cheese on top of each slice of bread. Then spoon some of the fried onions over the cheese.

5. Finish off the montadito by pouring a few drops of honey on top of the onion. Serve warm.

MONTADITO DE QUESO, UVAS Y NUECES

Montadito of Cottage Cheese with Grapes and Walnuts

This is a classical sweet and savoury tapa which contrasts the taste and texture of cheese with that of sweet grapes and thyme.

Ingredients:

> 4 slices of bread
> 24 white grapes
> 2 tablespoons of olive oil
> Half a teaspoon of thyme
> Freshly ground black pepper
> Salt
> 6 tablespoons of cottage cheese
> 4 walnuts, chopped roughly
> Fresh thyme to garnish

Preparation:

1. Coat the slices of bread with a little olive oil and toast them in an oven until they are golden and crisp.

2. Clean the grapes and sauté them in a frying pan with a little olive oil, adding thyme, pepper and salt. Keep stirring them so they don't brown too quickly.

3. When the grapes begin to turn brown, remove them from the heat.

4. Spread each slice of toast with cottage cheese (you can also add your own choice of herbs and spices to the cheese first).

5. Place the grapes on the cheese, pressing lightly to ensure that they do not fall off. Add some pieces of walnut and, finally, garnish with some fresh thyme.

6. Serve whilst the grapes are still hot.

PAN CATETO

Traditional Country Bread - Cateto

Traditionally, many country bar tapas are served on a slice of simple white bread. Here is a typical recipe for "Pan Cateto", the traditional country bread found in Andalucía and other parts of rural Spain. It's often used for breakfast, toasted with olive oil and tomato, but also fresh to serve various tapas. It is especially good with a little olive oil. It becomes hard quite quickly and is then often turned into breadcrumbs for use in other recipes.

Ingredients:

> 1 kg of bread flour (durum wheat "cateta")
> 585 ml of water,
> 20 g salt
> 8 g dry baker's yeast or a cube of 25 g fresh yeast

Preparation:

1. Weigh all the ingredients. Dissolve the yeast in water.

2. Put the flour in a large bowl, gradually add the yeast and water and mix with the flour until it is fully absorbed. Add salt and work it into the dough.

3. Knead the dough on a floured surface until smooth and elastic.

4. Take a clean bowl, rub some oil on the inside and put the dough in it. Cover the bowl with a damp cloth and let the dough rise until it has doubled in volume.

5. Take out the dough again and knead a little. Shape the dough into a ball.

6. Put baking paper on a baking tray and place the ball of dough on it. Cover it with a damp cloth and let it rise a second time until the dough has doubled in volume again.

7. Preheat the oven to 240°C. Make cuts on the surface of the bread dough with a sharp knife.

8. Quickly spray the dough with some water and put it into the hot oven. This will make a crispy crust. Bake for 10 minutes at 240°C.

9. After 10 minutes, reduce the temperature to 200°C and bake for another hour. Remove the bread and let it cool on a wire rack.

PAN CON TOMATE

Tomato Rubbed Bread

This simple dish can be found throughout Spain in many formats and with different names. It is often eaten at breakfast, but is also a favourite and tasty tapa or canapé.

In Cataluña it is called Pa amb tomàquet ('Bread with tomato') or in Mallorca pa amb oli ('Bread with olive oil'). In Mallorca, Pa amb oli is prepared with tomato called Tomàtiga de Ramallet, which is a specific variety of tomatoes on the vine, smaller and with a flavour a little bit more intense and sour than that of normal tomatoes.

The bread base used traditionally is a toasted slice of one of the dense country breads. Sometimes the tomato and garlic mix is pre-made and spread on the toast, when served as a canapé or tapa, but traditionally the diners add the tomato, garlic and olive oil themselves directly onto the toasted bread. It can be eaten by itself, but is often topped with cheese.

Ingredients:

> 8 slices of toasted pan cateto (country bread)
> 4 cloves of garlic, peeled and cut in half
> 2 large ripe tomatoes, cut in quarters
> Olive oil
> Chopped fresh parsley
> Salt

Preparation:

1. For canapés or small tapas, the bread can be cut into smaller slices or substituted with thin slices of baguette. It can be toasted or not, according to taste. We will describe the toasted version.

2. Take a piece of the toasted cateto and rub the cut edge of garlic over its surface.

3. Then rub the cut side of a tomato quarter on the toast until it softens with the tomato pulp. The tomato flesh will naturally stay on the toast.

4. Pour olive oil on top and sprinkle with salt and parsley to taste. Repeat with the remaining slices of toast and serve.

PAN REBOZADO AL AJILLO

Garlic Bread and Egg

This is a simple, savoury bread tapa which can be eaten alone or used as a basis for other tapas recipes.

Ingredients:

> 5 to 6 slices of bread
> 2 cloves of garlic
> 3 eggs
> Salt
> Black pepper
> Parsley to taste
> Olive oil

Preparation:

1. Peel and slice the garlic very thinly.

2. Beat the eggs, season with salt and pepper and add the sliced garlic. Put aside.

3. Cut the bread in slices about as thick as a finger, heat a frying pan with about 6 tablespoons of olive oil.

4. Dip the slices of bread in the egg so that they are well soaked and fry them until golden on both sides.

5. Remove the bread from the pan and drain on paper towels. Sprinkle with some chopped or dried parsley to taste. Serve warm.

TAPAS DE PAN DE SEMILLAS DE SESAMO

Tapas on Sesame seed Bread

Ingredients:

>Sesame seed bread
>Red peppers
>Green peppers
>Red tomatoes to spread on the bread
>Green tomatoes
>Boiled eggs
>Olive oil
>Vinegar

Preparation:

1. Put the red and green peppers into a tray, add some olive oil and grill them until cooked.

2. Cut the sesame bread into thick slices and spread them with the red tomato and some olive oil.

3. Cut the cooked peppers into thin strips and lay these on the bread. Add a slice of green tomato and a slice of hard boiled egg.

4. Finally, add a little olive oil and vinegar and serve.

TARTAR DE AGUACATE SOBRE TOSTA FINA DE PAN

Avocado Tartar on Toast

Ingredients:

>1 avocado
>1 medium-sized onion
>2 small tomatoes
>1 lemon
>5 large pickled gherkins
>3 tablespoons of olive oil
>2 tablespoons of tomato sauce
>5 drops of chilli sauce (tabasco)
>1 tablespoon of lemon juice
>Salt
>Pepper

Preparation:

1. Chop all the ingredients. Dice the avocado and tomato and very finely chop the onion and gherkins. If the tomatoes have a hard skin, it's best to blanch and skin them first. It may also be necessary to remove excess seeds.

2. Grate the skin of the lemon, taking care not to include the white part and juice half of the lemon. Add the lemon rind, the juice and the other remaining ingredients to the vegetable mix: tomato sauce, tabasco sauce, olive oil, and salt and pepper to taste.

3. Mix all the ingredients together and allow the mixture to marinate. The result should be thick. Cool the mixture before serving.

4. Serve on thin slices of toast.

TOSTADA DE HUEVOS DE CODORNIZ

Quails' Eggs with Cheese on Toast

Ingredients:

> 1 slice of toasted bread
> 2 quails' eggs
> Olive oil to fry
> Some grated cheese

Preparation:

1. Cut a slice of bread and toast it.

2. Fry the quails' eggs in a little olive oil.

3. When the eggs are fried, sprinkle on the cheese so it can melt. This needs to be done on a very low heat.

4. Place the eggs with the melted cheese on the toasted bread and serve.

TOSTAS

Spanish Toast

Tostas (Spanish toast) are the traditional pre-cursors of crackers. They are slices of bread which are brushed with olive oil and baked in the oven. They are the basis of many tapa and canapé recipes and generally used when cool. For instance, they are served rubbed with garlic, or with melted cheese or tomato as toppings. If the tostas are smallish, then one can make various tapas by, for example, adding a slice of tortilla, pâté, olives, etc.

Ingredients:

> 1 long loaf of bread, sliced diagonally, about 1.5 cm thick
> Olive oil

Preparation:

1. Pre-heat the oven to 190°C.

2. Brush the olive oil on each bread slice on one side only, making sure that you use enough oil to coat them properly.

3. Arrange the slices side by side on a shallow baking tray and bake for 6 minutes.

4. Turn the tray round in the oven and bake for a further 6 minutes.

5. Allow to cool.

TOSTAS DE ESPÁRRAGOS CON SALSA ROMESCO

Asparagus Spears in Romesco Sauce on Toast

Ingredients:

Slices of bread for toast
3 bunches of asparagus
4 cloves of garlic
2 or 3 dried red peppers (choriceros)
A few sprigs of parsley
2 small slices of bread
1 ripe tomato
50 g of roasted, peeled almonds
Vinegar
Salt
Olive oil
Cayenne pepper or chilli to taste (optional)

Preparation:

1. Begin by re-hydrating the peppers in water for 24 hours (warm water speeds up the process).

2. Remove any tough parts from the asparagus.

3. Fill a tall saucepan with enough salted water to cover the asparagus halfway. Tie up the asparagus with string into bunches and put them in the pan, standing upright. Boil for ten minutes.

4. After this time, cut the string and let the whole asparagus cook for another 10 minutes. This is done because the tips of the asparagus are much more tender than the stems. This way they get evenly cooked. When they are done, drain them and set them aside.

5. For the sauce, fry 3 whole garlic cloves (peeled) in plenty of oil and simmer until browned. Put them aside. In the same oil, fry the peppers and put aside. In the same oil fry the parsley and put aside. Then fry the small slices of bread and set aside. Finally fry the chopped tomato, again in the same oil.

6. Place all the fried ingredients in a blender, together with the almonds, the remaining peeled clove of garlic, a splash of vinegar, salt and olive oil. Add the chilli or paprika to your taste. Blend into a mayonnaise-like consistency, gradually adding more olive oil as needed.

If we see that the sauce is too thick (which is very likely) add a little water.

7. When the sauce is ready, fry the slices of bread very quickly on a very high heat on both sides until golden brown. This is done because the crusty fried bread remains crispy much longer than normal toast, which tends to soften quickly with the moisture from the asparagus and sauce.

8. Place three asparagus on each slice of bread and cover with a couple of tablespoons of the sauce. Sprinkle with chopped parsley and serve.

TOSTA DE QUESO CON ACEITUNAS Y MERMELADA DE TOMATE

Tosta with Cheese, Olives and Tomato Jam

Ingredients:

>200 g of cream cheese
>60 g olives (green or black), drained and finely chopped
>Rocket leaves
>4 slices of toasted bread
>Olive oil
>Tomato "jam" (see recipe Mermelada de Tomate)
>Sesame seed

Preparation:

1. Mix the cream cheese with the finely chopped olives in a bowl.

2. Place a piece of plastic shrink wrap on the kitchen surface and place the cream cheese onto the plastic to form a roll. Wrap the cheese up, expelling the air and mould it into a roll of about 8 centimetres long. Place it for an hour in the freezer, so that the cheese hardens.

3. Put the slices of toast onto a serving dish and cover them with some rocket leaves. Dress with a few drops of olive oil.

4. Take the cheese from the freezer, remove the cling film and cut 8 slices of about a centimetre thick.

5. Add a spoonful of tomato jam and finish off with a topping of sesame seed.

---o0o---

2.3 Pâtés

Pâtés are often served as a tapa on their own or with a slice of bread, toast or some bread sticks (of which there is a huge variety in Spain. A very popular type for pâté is a small round bread stick called a "pico").

There are at least as many vegetable pâtés as there are non-vegetarian types. Many of them have their origins in the culinary traditions of the Arabs and Jews. Some were created by the Christians as simple non-meat appetizers eaten on religious feast days, when they were required to abstain from meat.

PÂTÉ DE ACEITUNAS (OLIVADA)

Green or Black Olive Pâté (Tapenade)

This is a simple and savoury olive pâté: "tapenade". Here the recipe states green olives, but it can also be made with black olives.

Ingredients:

> 100 g of stoned green olives
> 1 tablespoon of the olive marinade water
> A quantity a little less than the olives of walnuts, pistachios, or peanuts
> 1 clove of garlic

Preparation:

1. Mix the olives and nuts; add the tablespoon of marinade and the chopped garlic.

2. Blend everything together until the mixture has a pâté consistency.

3. Correct the texture and consistency of the pâté with some breadcrumbs, if necessary.

4. Serve with toast.

PÂTÉ DE ALCACHOFAS

Artichoke Pâté

Ingredients:

> 3 artichokes
> 8 green olives
> Grated cheese
> Ground black pepper
> Vinegar of Jerez
> Salt to taste
> Olive oil

Preparation:

1. Clean and prepare the artichokes for cooking. Cut the hearts in quarters and cook them in boiling water until tender.

2. Drain the artichokes and put them in a blender with the remaining ingredients.

3. Blend into a smooth creamy pâté. Add some more salt, if necessary.

4. Keep a little grated cheese for garnish and serve the pâté with toast.

PÂTÉ DE BERENJENAS (BABA GANOUSH)
Aubergine Pâté (I)

This is a simple tapa recipe, very similar to "baba ganoush", the Levantine aubergine pâté that is so popular in North Africa and the Middle East, where it is served as a "mezze" - a Middle East variant of a tapa or aperitif. Clearly this recipe has its origins in Spain's historical links with Muslim and Jewish culinary tradition.

Ingredients:

> 0.5 kg of aubergines
> Olive oil
> 2-3 cloves of garlic
> 6 onions
> 3-4 sprigs of parsley
> Salt
> 2 teaspoons of vinegar
> Cateto bread or similar

Preparation:

1. Cut the aubergine into slices of approximately 1cm. thick. Pour a few tablespoons of olive oil into a large frying pan on a medium heat. When hot, add the aubergine and fry, stirring often.

2. While frying the aubergine, cut the onions, peel and finely chop the garlic cloves.

3. When the aubergine is soft and browned on all sides (after about 10 minutes), remove from the pan and allow it to cool on a plate.

4. Pour some more olive oil into the same frying pan. Sauté the onions and garlic for about 3 to 5 minutes. Remove from frying pan and place in a blender, adding vinegar, parsley and the aubergine slices. Blend until the pâté is smooth. Add salt to your taste.

5. Serve warm in a bowl as a tapa or spread the pâté on slices of cateto bread or toast. Note: If you want to make your aubergine pâté taste like traditional Levantine "baba ganoush", then add a little sesame paste (tahini), cumin (1 teaspoons of each) and the juice of half a lemon. Adjust these quantities to your taste.

PÂTÉ DE BERENJENAS

Aubergine Pâté (II)

This is another recipe for aubergine pâté, this time using the skin of aubergines to make the pâté. This can be useful if you happen to use the aubergine flesh for another recipe and would normally have discarded the skins.

Ingredients:

Skin of 5 aubergines
1 onion
1 large tomato
3 tablespoons of raw almonds
10 black pitted olives
Salt
Olive oil

Preparation:

1. Wash the aubergines well, peel them and chop up the skins. Chop up the onion.

2. Fry the aubergine skins and onion together in a little olive oil.

3. Skin the tomatoes and cut them into small pieces. Add these to the frying pan. When the sauce is almost cooked, add the almonds and let them fry a little. Next add the black olives and leave it all to cook for a couple of minutes more.

4. When everything is cooked through, put the mixture into the blender and blend until it has the consistency of a pâté. Add salt to taste.

5. Serve warm or cold. The pâté can be served as a tapa by itself or with bread or toast.

PÂTÉ DE CALABACÍN Y NUEZ

Courgette and Walnut Pâté

This traditional Andaluz recipe has its origins in Arabic cuisine, where it is known as "Mtabbal kousa". There are many variations of the recipe, for example using cheese or yogurt, and different herbs, including mint.

Ingredients:

> 1 courgette
> 1 teaspoon of olive oil
> 1 tablespoon of breadcrumbs
> 1 dozen walnuts
> 1 pinch of salt

Preparation:

1. Peel and roast the courgette.

2. Blend all the ingredients together in a blender.

3. Serve on toast or bread, accompanied by pieces of walnut and sprinkled with fresh mint.

Note: A similar courgette pâté can be made by adding cream cheese during the blending. In this case, add about 50% of the weight of the courgette in cream cheese.

PÂTÉ DE CHAMPIÑONES

Mushroom Pâté

Ingredients:

> 1 medium-sized onion
> 0.5 kg of mushrooms
> Olive oil
> 150 g of breadcrumbs
> 1 clove of garlic
> Nutmeg
> Oregano and basil to taste
> Salt and pepper to taste
> Juice of half a lemon

Preparation:

1. Finely chop the onion and the mushrooms.

2. Sauté the onion in some olive oil until golden. Add the mushrooms and cook for a couple of minutes.

3. Moisten the breadcrumbs with some hot water and add this to the mushrooms and onions, together with the lemon juice and crushed garlic. Simmer the mixture until the liquid is reduced.

4. Remove from the heat and add nutmeg, salt, pepper, oregano and basil to taste.

5. Blend this mixture until it has the consistency of a thick paste. Add breadcrumbs or olive oil to adjust the consistency.

6. Place in a serving bowl, cover with plastic wrap and refrigerate.

7. This pâté is usually served on tostas or crackers, garnished with sliced raw mushrooms.

PÂTÉ DE CHAMPIÑONES Y PIMIENTOS

Mushroom and Pepper Pâté

Ingredients:

>500 g of mushrooms
>1 large onion
>2 green peppers
>Olive oil
>Juice of half a lemon
>Breadcrumbs
>Fresh basil
>Fresh parsley
>Oregano
>Salt and pepper to taste

Preparation:

1. Wash and chop the mushrooms, onion and peppers into small pieces.

2. Fry all these ingredients in a little olive oil.

3. Once the vegetables are cooked, add a pinch of salt and the parsley, oregano, basil and lemon juice.

4. Put all the ingredients into a blender and blend together, gradually adding breadcrumbs until obtaining the smooth consistency of a pâté.

5. Allow the pâté to cool and serve it spread on toast or bread.

PÂTÉ DE ESPÁRRAGOS

Asparagus Pâté

Ingredients:

> 2 bunches of asparagus - white or green
> 0.5 litre of cream
> 6 eggs
> Salt and pepper to taste

Preparation:

1. Cut the asparagus into pieces and cook them in the cream.

2. When they come to the boil, remove them and put them in the blender with the eggs, salt and pepper. If you use green asparagus, you will need to cook them a bit longer before they are tender.

3. Grease a baking tin mould with butter and cover the bottom with aluminium foil or baking paper. Pour the asparagus mixture into the tin.

4. Cook the pâté in a water bath in a preheated oven at 180ºC for 40 minutes (or until a cocktail stick pushed into the pate comes out clean).

5. The pâté can be served warm with a béchamel sauce to which we can add a little tomato sauce, or served cold with a mayonnaise sauce - whipped mayonnaise with a splash of cream - or it can be served by itself. As a tapa it is often served with bread or tostas.

PÂTÉ DE GARBANZOS Y LIMÓN

Chickpea Pâté

Chickpeas are grown in Spain and widely used in many stews and meal soup recipes. This is a recipe which uses them to make a pâté. Although this dish is very similar to Middle Eastern hummus, this pâté has a more Spanish flavour. It can be served as a tapa by itself, on bread or toast, or as a dip.

Ingredients:

> 500 g of cooked chickpeas
> 150 ml of olive oil
> 250 ml of lemon juice
> 200 g of chopped red onion
> 2 cloves of garlic
> 1 tablespoon of dried parsley
> Salt and pepper to taste

Preparation:

1. Put the cooked chickpeas, the red onion and salt and pepper to taste all together into the blender. Blend until all the ingredients are thoroughly mixed.

2. Add the lemon juice and olive oil. Blend again. The final mixture should be a thick, creamy paste.

3. Finally add the parsley and garlic and blend again.

4. Check the taste and add salt and pepper, if required

5. Garnish with an olive and serve as a cold tapa, either by itself or with bread or toast.

PÂTÉ DE HABAS Y MENTA

Pâté of Broad Beans and Mint

Ingredients:

> 100 g of fresh broad beans
> 25 g of walnuts
> 1 sprig of fresh mint
> 1 teaspoon of olive oil
> 1 pinch of salt

Preparation:

1. Steam the beans for 10 minutes.

2. Blend the beans and the other ingredients in a blender until obtaining a fine paste.

3. Store in the refrigerator.

4. Serve this pâté alone as a tapa, or spread on pieces of bread or toast.

PÂTÉ DE JUDÍAS BLANCAS Y LIMA

White Bean and Lime Pâté

Ingredients:

> 400 g of cooked white beans
> 50 g of chopped almonds
> Juice of 1 lime
> 1 clove of garlic
> Salt to taste
> 100 ml of olive oil
> 1 tablespoon of chopped oregano

Preparation:

1. If the beans are from a jar, rinse them before use.

2. Put the beans in a blender with the lime juice, garlic and almonds and blend the mixture until it becomes a thick and creamy paste. Gradually add olive oil to achieve a softer consistency.

3. Manually stir in the oregano.

4. Season with salt, if necessary.

5. The pâté can be served as a tapa by itself, or with bread, toast or bread sticks.

PÂTÉ DE PIMIENTOS VERDES

Green Pepper Pâté

This is a traditional recipe which can be made with either fried or boiled green peppers. Normally the dish is made using breadcrumbs, but here we have used ground almonds instead.

Ingredients:

> 500 g of green peppers
> 6 tablespoons of ground almonds (or 6 tablespoons of breadcrumbs)
> 1 pinch of salt

Preparation:

1. Remove the stems and seeds from the peppers. Boil them over medium heat for about 10 minutes.

2. Blend the peppers, the ground almonds (or breadcrumbs) and a little salt together in a blender until it has the consistency of a pâté.

3. Cool the pâté in the fridge and serve as a tapa alone, or with bread or toast.

PÂTÉ DE TOMATES SECOS

Pâté of Dried Tomatoes

This is a very simple recipe for a tasty raw pâté combining the intense flavour of dried tomatoes with a hint of almond.

Ingredients:

> 15 dried tomatoes
> 5 tablespoons of raw almonds
> Juice of half a lemon
> 1 clove of garlic
> 3 tablespoons of olive oil

Preparation:

1. Put the dried tomatoes in a bowl together with the olive oil and let them marinate for 10-12 hours.

2. Squeeze the lemon and put the juice aside.

3. Peel and crush the garlic with a mortar and pestle.

4. Put the tomatoes and oil into the blender and add the garlic, lemon juice, the peeled almonds and a little warm water.

5. Blend the mixture thoroughly; adding more water if needed to obtain a thick, consistent paste.

6. Chill the mixture in the refrigerator.

7. Serve as a tapa with fresh bread, toast or a cracker.

PÂTÉ DE ZANAHORIAS

Carrot Pâté

This is a tasty carrot, walnut and basil pâté that can be used as a tapa spread on bread or toast, or even as a side dish. This recipe is also traditional in other Mediterranean countries, like Tunisia, for example, where it is often eaten during Ramadan (because it can be prepared in advance). In the Tunisian version, the recipe includes tahini (sesame paste) and is spiced with cumin instead of containing nuts and basil.

Ingredients:

> 2 large carrots
> 2 large cloves of garlic
> Olive oil
> 200 ml of walnuts
> Fresh basil
> Salt to taste

Preparation:

1. Wash and cook the unpeeled carrots.

2. When the carrots are tender, put them in a blender with all the other ingredients. Use plenty of olive oil to obtain a very creamy consistency, and add basil and salt to your taste.

3. Serve cold as a tapa with bread sticks, or spread the pâté on toast.

---oOo---

2.4 Pickles, Marinades, Jams, and Conserves

In Spain, pickled gherkins, pearl onions, garlic, olives and other pickled vegetables are known as "encurtidos", and they are officially defined in the dictionary of the Royal Academy of Spain as "fruits or vegetables that are preserved by keeping them in vinegar".

The evolution of pickling vegetables is ancient, having begun in India about 2000 BC. The technique of pickling to preserve vegetables was brought to Spain by the Romans and later by the Arab colonists to preserve foods beyond their season and during long sea and land shipments; especially at high temperatures when fresh products spoil very quickly.

Nowadays, these sour, salty, sweet and crunchy pickled foods are very common in Spanish gastronomy. They are present at every social occasion, are widely consumed as tapas, used in traditional recipes, and even in some of the country's most avant-garde cuisine.

Cold marinated tapas are especially popular in Spain during the hot summer months. Many a bar will have a tapa display with various cold tapas. Their regional variety reflects Spain's agricultural diversity, the rich localised gastronomic traditions, and the links between modern Spanish food and many truly ancient traditional foods.

Some of these recipes are not tapa dishes in themselves, but they are commonly used to make other tapa dishes and are referred to elsewhere in this book.

ACEITUNAS ALIÑADO

Marinated Olives

There are as many recipes for marinating olives as there are families in Spain. So, here we are going to give you an idea of how the basic process works; with some suggestions and a couple of variations.

Most olives in Spain are marinated when they are still green, rather than black. Marinating black olives tends to be more common in parts of Portugal and in some parts of Northern Spain, like Aragón).

Ancient and Modern Methods: Marinating olives in the traditional way does not use any chemicals (apart from salt). Modern industrial olive production, however, uses Sodium Hydroxide (caustic soda) to leech the bitterness from the raw olives. Nonetheless, we recommend that you use only water, or brine. It serves the same purpose, is a little bit slower, but it leaves the olive fruit with much more of its natural flavour and nutrients and it is better for your health and the environment.

Harvesting and Preparation: Any olive can be marinated, but the best olives (from an eating point of view) are those which have plenty of "flesh" on them. On the other hand, some very interesting results can also be obtained using smaller olives with proportionately large stones. There are several classical eating olives in Spain. The type which is most often seen commercially is known as "manzanilla" - the little apple. It is a round olive with a small stone. There are also some giant varieties around, generally from the area around Sevilla, which is famous for its large table olives ("gordos": fat ones).

At the trees: It is important to harvest table olives carefully, so they are usually hand-picked or raked from the tree into fruit trays. They should be in perfect condition and not broken or bruised.

Sorting: Remove the leaves and branches from the olives. Discard any bruised or insect-damaged fruit. Put the good fruit straight into a large barrel of fresh water. Ideally, the water should not be very chlorinated, as this can affect the taste of the olive. On the other hand, the water needs to be sterile to avoid introducing moulds into the process. When the harvest is fully sorted, wash it thoroughly with fresh water, gently stirring the olives around to loosen any dirt. Repeat the washing and sorting process 3 or 4 times, until you end up with a batch of clean olives.

Stoning or splitting: In order to leach the bitterness from the olives, it is better to "break" them to let the water get into the flesh. Alternatively, you can just remove the stone from the olives before marinating them. Small hand-held machines are available cheaply to do this.

If you decide to leave the stone, you can either "break" the olive with an olive mallet or use another ingenious wooden tool with tiny blades that insert 4 small cuts in the olive skin. In either case, the olives need to be prepared for leeching. When they are either stoned or broken, they should be rinsed again.

The leeching process: There are several ways of doing this. Generally you need to have some food grade plastic drums for this purpose which are large enough to accommodate the quantity of olives you are making and allowing for plenty of water (allow a minimum of 1 to 5, olives to water). The traditional method uses large earthenware pots.

The most simple and common traditional leeching method is to steep the olives in water (keep them under water with a weighted lid) and then just to rinse out the olives with fresh water once or twice per day, replacing the steeping water with completely fresh water. This process of changing the water is repeated until the olives show no sign of bitterness. This can take several weeks.

An alternative method uses a salt mix. Add enough salt to the leeching water to float an egg on it (note how much salt this is) and use this salted water to leech the olives. Change the water (and salt) every one or two days, until the olives have lost their bitterness. This process is a bit faster than using just water.

Marination: This is where the art of olive making really begins. When the olives have lost their bitterness, it is time to marinate them in preparation for storage and eating.

There is an infinite number of marinades possible. However, the basis of all marinades is a salt solution to which you should add some acidic component, like vinegar and/or lemon juice (acids inhibit bacterial growth in food). Then add the herbs and spices you like. Most people add garlic, thyme, oregano and rosemary. Some people add chilli peppers. Many traditional recipes add some other interesting and edible components like slices of orange, lemon, carrot, green and red peppers, etc. Traditionally, the herbs that are added to the marinade are those that grow wild in the area.

Once you have chosen your marinade recipe, the leeched olives are packed into the marinade, ensuring that the olives are fully covered at all times. Traditionally, olives were kept in the marinade in earthenware vessels with wooden lids, but you can also store your olives in glass jars (sterile "kilner" jars will work, but wash them well on the outside after filling). Olives tend to ferment - which is fine - and the marinade is salty and slightly acid and may corrode metal lids, so be aware of this. The ideal solution is to use the traditional earthenware container and keep the olives in a cool place. They are ready to eat after a few weeks when they have softened and taken on the flavours of the marinade. After that, they just get better with time.

RECETAS DE ACEITUNAS ALIÑADAS
Recipes for Olive Marinades

Whether you make your own marinated olives or simply buy olives ready to eat, it's nice to use different marinades to alter the flavour of the olives. Many "supermarket" olives are fairly bland. To restore a more traditional taste to them, a homemade marinade is perfect.

There are a limitless number of possible marinades - everyone in Spain will have their own family favourite. Here we have suggested some recipes for making your own marinades. You can then experiment with different tastes.

To make your own marinated olives, you need to buy olives which have not already been strongly marinated, so that the olives will take on the taste of your marinade, rather than add a new set of tastes to an existing marinated olive. So for this, choose an olive that has a neutral taste.

It's worth noting that the marinades we describe here can also be used as a salad dressing, so there is no need to throw them away after serving your olives.

ACEITUNAS ADOBADAS AL HINOJO

Marinated Olives with Fennel

Ingredients:

200 g of green and/or black olives
75 g fennel bulb
A few sprigs of fennel
6 coriander seeds
1 clove of garlic
1 tablespoon of olive oil
1 tablespoon of lemon juice
Salt and black pepper to taste

Preparation:

1. Drain the olives and place them in a bowl. Cut the fennel bulb into thin slices. Wash the olives, the fennel bulb and leaf.

2. Grind the coriander seeds in a mortar and add them to the olives. Peel and finely chop the garlic and mix it together into a dressing with the olive oil and lemon juice.

3. Season the dressing with salt and freshly ground pepper.

4. Pour the dressing over the olives and stir all the ingredients together well.

5. Place the olives and marinade in a glass container (like a kilner jar) and leave the mix to marinate for at least 48 hours before serving.

ACEITUNAS CON ALMENDRAS Y SALSA ROMESCO

Olives with Almonds and Romesco Sauce

Ingredients:

>250 g of green olives
>4 tablespoons of romesco sauce (see recipe in the chapter about "Sauces...")
>3 tablespoons of blanched almonds
>1 tomato
>1 tablespoon of cider vinegar

Preparation:

1. Coarsely chop the almonds with a knife.

2. Mix the vinegar with the romesco sauce, the almonds and the olives.

3. Peel the tomato and chop it into small pieces. Add these to the olives and serve.

ACEITUNAS GORDAL RELLENAS DE QUESO CON TOMATE

Gordal Olives stuffed with Cheese and Tomato

Gordal olives are very large olives. This means they can be easily stuffed with a variety of fillings. Here we give a recipe for gordal olives stuffed with a sauce called "Almogrote", which is a delicious traditional sauce of the island of La Gomera in the Islas Canarias, made with cheese and tomatoes.

Ingredients:

> 250 g of stoned gordal olives
> 50 g of hard cheese
> 1 medium-sized tomato
> 2 tablespoons of tomato purée
> 2 tablespoons of chopped parsley
> Paprika powder to taste
> Cayenne pepper to taste
> 2 tablespoons of sweet wine
> 50 ml of olive oil

Preparation:

1. Cut the cheese into pieces and blend it together with the fresh tomato and the tomato purée.

2. The sauce has to be a thick, creamy paste. If it is too thick, add a little more tomato. If it is too liquid, add more cheese. Season the sauce with some cayenne pepper and sweet paprika to your taste.

3. Using a pastry bag, fill the olives with the cheese and tomato paste.

4. Just before eating the olives, put the olive oil with the wine and parsley in a glass jar. Cover it, shake it for a while until the mix is emulsified, pour the marinade over the olives and serve.

ACEITUNAS MANZANILLA CON NARANJA, JENGIBRE Y CILANTRO

Manzanilla Olives with Orange, Ginger and Coriander

The Manzanilla olive ("Manzanilla" means little apple) is a medium-sized round olive with a small stone. The marinade in this recipe has a light, spicy citrus flavour.

Ingredients:

>250 g of Manzanilla olives in brine
>Half an orange (use organic oranges because you will need the skin)
>1 fresh red chilli pepper (or less, according to your taste)
>A sprig of coriander
>5 coriander seeds
>Fresh ginger
>50 ml of olive oil

Preparation:

1. Grate the orange skin, being careful to avoid grating the pith. Squeeze the orange until you have 2 tablespoons of juice.

2. Lightly toast the coriander seeds and then grind them up in a mortar and pestle.

3. Grate a teaspoonful of peeled ginger.

4. Cut the chilli pepper into slices.

5. Put all the ingredients with the olives in a jar, mix well and leave to marinate in the refrigerator for 3 to 4 days.

6. Before serving, add some chopped fresh coriander leaves.

ACEITUNAS NEGRAS CON LIMÓN, HINOJO Y AJO

Black Olives with Lemon, Garlic and Fennel

Aragón is well-known for its black olives. Fennel is a common wild herb in Spain and is often used as part of an olive marinade. Garlic and olives naturally go very well together and when all these tastes are mixed together with a lemon flavour, this marinade makes for a very tasty combination.

Ingredients:

>   250 g of black olives (of Aragón)
>   Half a lemon (preferably organic because you will use the skin as well)
>   2 cloves of garlic
>   Some sprigs of fennel
>   Dried oregano
>   75 ml of olive oil

Preparation:

1. Clean the lemon and cut it into small pieces without peeling.

2. Peel the garlic cloves and cut them in half, vertically.

3. Cut the sprigs of fennel into thin slices, and chop the leaves.

4. Mix the herbs and lemon with the olives in a large jar, stir for half a minute to lightly crush the lemon, add the olive oil and stir again.

5. Keep the olives in the refrigerator for about 3 or 4 days to marinate.

AJOS MARINADOS

Marinated Garlic

Marinated garlic has a very delicate flavour, almost like almonds, and they are easier to digest. They make a very tasty tapa together with, for example, chopped capers, olives, finely chopped peppers and oregano on a "tosta" and can also be used as seasoning in a pasta dish.

Ingredients:

> 400 ml of white wine vinegar
> 4 heads of garlic
> 3 bay leaves
> 3 cloves
> Salt and pepper
> 1 glass of white wine
> 1 teaspoon of sugar

Preparation:

1. Peel the cloves of garlic.

2. Put the vinegar in a saucepan with the spices and boil for 3 minutes.

3. Add the salt and sugar and bring back to the boil.

4. Add the cloves of garlic and let them boil in the vinegar mix for 2 or 3 minutes.

5. Now put the garlic cloves into sterilised kilner jars and cover them with the vinegar and spice mix. Seal the jars.

6. Let the garlic marinate for one month before eating.

ALCAPARRAS

Pickled Capers

The caper is a perennial deciduous plant with beautiful, large white to pinkish-white flowers. It is best known for the edible flower buds (capers), which are usually consumed pickled. The buds, when ready to pick, are a dark olive green and range in size from the size of a fresh kernel of corn to the size of a small olive. The plant has an ancient history and there are several claims about its health benefits. It grows wild in many parts of Spain.

Ingredients:

> 250 grams of fresh capers (tapenas)
> 1 teaspoon of salt
> 4 tablespoons of vinegar
> Water

Preparation:

1. Collect the capers early in the morning before the flowers open.

2. Remove the stems (optionally) and wash the capers well, drain them and put them in a sterile glass jar. Add the salt and vinegar, cover with water, and stir well.

3. Close the jar and leave it for a couple of days in the sun. After that, it is ready to store somewhere dark and cool.

4. After 2 weeks of marination, the capers are ready to eat. Prepared in this way, they can be stored for a very long time (at least a year).

5. Serve as a tapa alone, or with olives and some cheese.

MERMELADA DE TOMATE

Tomato Jam

Ingredients (for 1 small jar):

500 g peeled and seeded tomatoes (roughly 1 kg of unpeeled tomatoes)
125 g of brown sugar
125 g of white sugar
50 ml of lemon juice

Preparation:

1. Clean, skin and deseed the tomatoes. Chop them into small pieces.

2. Check the weight of the tomatoes. Use approximately half of the weight of the tomatoes in sugar. Therefore, for 500 g of tomatoes use 250 g of sugar in total.

3. Mix the tomatoes well with the sugar and let the mixture stand for 30 minutes.

4. Put the tomato and sugar mix in a saucepan. Add the lemon juice and place on a medium heat for 10 minutes. Remove any foam which forms.

5. Bring the mix to the boil for 5 minutes stirring constantly to avoid burning. This is important to kill any possible bacteria in our jam.

6. Turn down the heat and leave to simmer for 20 or 30 minutes until the jam has the right consistency: moist but not wet, but not too thick either.

7. Remove the jam from the heat and let it cool slightly.

8. Make sure you have a sterilised jar ready. Fill it to the brim and seal it.

9. The jam will last for a long time in a fridge or other cold dark place. After opening, be careful to reseal the jar and keep it refrigerated.

10. The jam is delightful served as a tapa with bread or toast and combines very well with a good cheese like manchego, or a strong goats' cheese.

PIMIENTOS ROJOS Y QUESO MANCHEGO

Marinated Red Peppers and Manchego Cheese

The combination of Manchego cheese, grilled red peppers and olive oil is very pleasant and a little slice of each, marinated overnight, makes an excellent traditional tapa. Any good mature Spanish sheep or goats' cheese can be used as a substitute for Manchego.

Ingredients:

> 2 medium-sized red peppers
> 250 g of Manchego cheese, cut into 12 triangles
> 3 tablespoons of olive oil
> 1 large clove of garlic, finely sliced
> Half a teaspoon of cumin seed

Preparation:

1. Clean and de-seed the peppers. Cut them into strips.

2. Grill them with a little olive oil until they begin to brown.

3. Arrange the cheese triangles on a round dish. Place 1 strip of pepper on each cheese slice.

4. Mix the olive oil with the garlic and the cumin seeds together in a bowl, and season with salt and pepper.

5. Spoon this marinade over and around the cheese with pepper.

6. Cover the dish and refrigerate overnight to blend the flavours.

7. Bring up to room temperature before serving with small slices of bread.

VINAGRETA DE LIMÓN Y ORÉGANO

Lemon and Oregano Vinaigrette

This is a salad dressing in which most of the vinegar is replaced by lemon juice.

Ingredients:

> 8 tablespoons of olive oil
> 3 tablespoons of lemon juice
> 1 tablespoon of white wine vinegar
> 1/2 teaspoon of dried oregano
> 1/2 teaspoon of salt

Preparation:

1. To prepare the vinaigrette, mix all the ingredients in a bowl, until well combined. It is then ready to be used

---oOo---

2.5 Soups, Creams, Sorbets, Purées, Porras, and Sauces

In this chapter we take a look at the vast range of traditional recipes for soups, creams, sorbets, porras and sauces served as tapas or as part of a tapa.

Let us first look at the culinary tradition of these dishes.

Sorbets: The sorbet was introduced into Europe during the Arab period of Al-Andalus. It had long been known in Arabia and along the silk route from trade contacts in China. From around the year 850 CE, the Moors of Granada stored ice and snow from the Sierra Nevada to mix with fruit to make their sorbets. Indeed, the word "sorbet" comes from the Arabic "srab", meaning drink.

The sorbet is best known as a frozen dessert. It differs from ice cream because it does not usually contain fatty ingredients like cream or egg. For this reason it has a less firm and creamy texture than ice cream. Ice cream as it is known today made its first European appearance in the seventeenth century. Sorbets have a much older tradition. The main ingredients of a sweet sorbet are fruit juices, sometimes a wine, brandy or liqueur, to which syrup or honey is added. However, sorbets are also often made with savoury ingredients in Spain, in the same way as gazpachos, and are a refreshing appetizer in the intense Spanish summers.

Gazpachos - Cold Soups: Gazpacho is a vegetable soup, traditionally served cold, originating in the southern Spanish region of Andalucía. It is normally a tomato-based soup, but there are many other gazpachos based on other vegetables. Gazpacho is very popular in Spain but also in Portugal, where it is known as "gaspacho".

Gazpacho is mostly consumed during the hot summer months, because of its refreshing qualities. Gazpacho has a long history. There are many theories about its origins. Some claim that it is originally an Arab soup made of bread, olive oil, water and garlic that arrived in Spain and Portugal with the Moors. Other food historians claim that it came to Spain via the Romans, with the addition of vinegar. Once in Spain, it became a popular part of Andalucían rural and urban cuisine, using stale bread, garlic, olive oil, salt and vinegar. There are many traditional and modern variations of gazpacho, often in different

94

colours, with and without tomatoes and bread. These variants include avocados, cucumbers, parsley, watermelon, grapes and asparagus.

Gazpachos are often served as tapas because they are very simple to make and very tasty. They can be served with or without meat or egg toppings and so they suit almost everyone's taste and food preferences.

Soups and Creams: Spain is famous for its soups. These range from simple, thin, light soups through to rich, thick, full-meal soups.

The definition of a soup in Spain implies that it is not enriched with cream or other creamy ingredients. A "cream" on the other hand refers to a soup which is blended, thickened and enriched using milk, cream, or yoghurt. Some "creams" also take advantage of the addition of olive oil and the natural creamy texture of the ingredients. As a tapa, they are usually served in small earthenware bowls and decorated with some herbs. Soup and cream tapas are often served with fresh, toasted bread or croutons.

Purées and Porras: There is a fine line between a soup, a cream, a purée, a porra and a pâté. Let us try to understand the differences.

A porra is a very thick, but very fine-textured paste. The word porra could be translated as "porridge", but the texture is much too smooth to be referred to in that way. Porras are often eaten alone or accompanied with various toppings (hard boiled egg, for example) or with bread or toast.

A purée is also a very thick paste, but it can be either fine-textured or it can be quite chunky. A purée is different from a pâté in that a pâté is generally thicker and is usually eaten as a spread on bread or some other base, whereas a purée is eaten alone or used as a dip for bread, toast, etc.

Sauces: Many tapas use various sauces and in this chapter we have also included recipes for Spanish traditional vegetarian versions of these sauces.

AJOBLANCO DE ALMENDRAS

Garlic Soup with Almonds

Ingredients:

>200 g of almonds (shelled)
>100 g slice of country bread (cateto)
>2 cloves of garlic
>1 bunch of muscatel grapes
>1.5 litre of water
>2 tablespoons of sherry vinegar
>250 ml of olive oil
>Salt (to taste)

Preparation:

1. Blanch the almonds in boiling water for a moment to remove their skin.

2. In a bowl, soak the bread in some water.

3. Grind the almonds, garlic and salt in a mortar with a pestle.

4. When well ground, add the bread and continue mashing whilst gradually adding the olive oil until you obtain a smooth, white paste and cannot distinguish any of the ingredients.

5. Slowly dissolve the paste in water, stirring continuously and prevent it from getting too watery.

6. When it reaches the desired consistency, add a dash of vinegar and serve chilled with some muscatel grapes.

AJOBLANCO DE MÁLAGA

Garlic Soup with Almonds of Málaga

Ingredients:

> 1 kg of blanched almonds
> 2.5 litre water
> 1 medium-sized loaf of bread in crumbs
> Olive oil
> Vinegar (to taste)
> Salt (to taste)
> 1 clove of garlic

Preparation:

1. Blend together the almonds, the breadcrumbs, a little water, oil, salt, vinegar and garlic.

2. The soup paste should be thick. If it is too thick or not thick enough then add a little more oil or almonds. Put it in the fridge to cool.

3. Before serving, add cold water to the soup paste and stir until it has the consistency you prefer.

4. Serve it cold in the summer or at room temperature in the winter, accompanied with muscatel grapes, pieces of apple or melon. It is often served in a small glass as a tapa.

AJOBLANCO CON GRANIZADO DE MUSCATEL

Garlic Soup with Almonds and Iced Muscatel

This is a favourite cold soup of Andalucía served during the hot summer months as a refreshing tapa.

Ingredients:

> 4 cloves of garlic
> 200 g peeled almonds
> 100 g breadcrumbs from stale bread (cateto)
> 200 ml olive oil
> Sherry vinegar
> Salt
> 1 litre of very cold water

For the iced muscatel:

> 200 g of Muscat grapes
> 500 g of red wine
> 1 glass of muscatel wine
> 200 g of sugar
> A squirt of vanilla essence

Preparation:

1. The ajoblanco: Put garlic and the almonds in a saucepan with 0.5 litre of water and boil for about 8 minutes. Remove with a draining spoon, cool in iced water and repeat the process until all the almonds and garlic are cooked.

2. Blend the almonds and garlic together in a blender for several minutes until obtaining a smooth paste.

3. While blending, gradually add the olive oil (as you would when making a mayonnaise).

4. Next add water, also very slowly, and finally add vinegar (to taste).

5. Pass the mixture through a purée mill and put aside.

6. The iced muscatel: Take a saucepan and boil all of the ingredients together for 5 minutes.

7. Let the pan cool and purée the mixture in a blender.

8. Pass the mixture through a purée mill and then pour it in ice cube moulds.

9. Put the moulds in the freezer for half an hour, then take them out and work the mixture with a spoon, to form the frappé ice.

10. Repeat the process a few times until you have the desired consistency. Store it in the freezer.

11. Serve the chilled garlic soup in a glass, together with the iced muscatel.

AJOBLANCO CON UVAS

Garlic Soup with Grapes

Ajoblanco was first created by the Moors. The combination of fresh fruit and dried fruit was classical Moorish culinary practice and this became one of the most popular dishes of the time. Ajoblanco remains one of only two white soups worldwide in which no dairy product is used.

Cold soups are particularly popular in Andalucía because they are quite refreshing during the long hot summers and they are also very simple and easy to make. They are the basic sustenance of the workers out in the field, tending the vineyards or harvesting the grapes. Ajoblanco, taken together with a few fresh grapes, makes a delicious, refreshing and nutritious dish.

The popularity of this particular cold soup, so the story goes, spread during the late nineteenth century. It became popular outside of the area when an engineer, who was working in the countryside of the province of Málaga, asked a local woman for some water. Instead, she made the man some Ajoblanco. He was so impressed by the taste and simplicity of the dish that when he returned to Madrid, he publicised the dish in glowing reports.

Ingredients:

> 90 g of blanched almonds
> 3 cloves of garlic, peeled
> 1/2 teaspoon of salt
> 4 slices of stale white bread, crusts removed
> 1 l of iced water
> 7 tablespoons of olive oil
> 3 tablespoons of white wine vinegar
> 2 tablespoons of sherry vinegar
> 1 tablespoon of butter
> 6 slices of white bread, crusts removed, cut in cubes
> 225 g seedless green grapes

Preparation:

1. Grind the almonds, 2 of the garlic cloves and salt to a fine consistency in a blender.

2. Soak the stale bread in 250 ml of iced water, then squeeze to extract moisture. Add the bread to the blender.

3. With the blender running, add 6 tablespoons of olive oil and 250 ml of iced water slowly in a steady stream.

4. Add the vinegars and mix on high speed for 2 minutes.

5. Pour the mixture into a bowl. Add the remaining water and mix well. Adjust seasonings with salt and vinegar. Chill for up to 6 hours.

Optional - croutons:

6. Heat the butter with the remaining oil in a pan.

7. Crush a garlic clove and fry it with the bread cubes, tossing to coat.

8. Cook over a very low heat, stirring occasionally, for 20-30 minutes or until cubes are golden.

9. Serve the soup ice cold, garnished with the croutons and fresh grapes.

ALIOLI

Garlic Mayonnaise

Homemade garlic mayonnaise is often served in Spain as part of a tapa, or alone with bread or as a side sauce with various potato or vegetable tapas.

Ingredients:

> 2 eggs
> 0.25 teaspoon of Dijon mustard
> 1 teaspoon of salt
> 2 tablespoons of lemon juice
> 120 ml of olive oil
> 120 ml of vegetable oil
> 2 cloves of garlic, crushed

Preparation:

1. Put 1 egg and the yolk of the other egg in the bowl of a food processor. Discard the white of the 2nd egg (use for something else). Add the mustard, the salt and the lemon juice.

2. Blend well, but slowly. Very gradually add the oil in a steady stream. When all oil is used, you should have a thick and glossy mayonnaise.

3. Stir in the garlic, mix well and serve with a light sprinkling of parsley.

ALIOLI DE ZANAHORIA

Carrot Garlic Sauce

"Alioli" comes from the Catalan "all i oli", meaning garlic and oil. Alioli is a very popular sauce in the Mediterranean cuisine. This version uses carrots as its base rather than eggs.

Ingredients:

> 2 carrots
> 2 cloves of garlic
> Oregano (to taste)
> Salt (to taste)
> Lemon juice
> Olive oil

Preparation:

1. Cook the 2 carrots and then blend them with a little water, the garlic, salt and a squeeze of lemon juice.

2. Continue to blend slowly and gradually add the olive oil until you get a mayonnaise-like texture.

3. Finally, mix in some oregano to taste.

4. Serve cool with croutons as a tapa, or as part of other tapas recipes which use alioli.

ALMOGROTE

Almogrote - Tomato and Cheese Spread of La Gomera

Almogrote is a soft paste made from hard cheese, tomatoes, olive oil, garlic, and spices, which is typically eaten spread on toast. It is native to La Gomera, one of the Islas Canarias. The best cheese to use is the slightly spicy queso duro gomero (Gomera hard cheese), but you can use any aged or medium aged goats' cheese.

Ingredients:

>500 g of ripe tomatoes
>2 cloves of garlic
>Olive oil
>500 g of mature cheese
>2 teaspoons of paprika powder
>A pinch of pepper

Preparation:

1. Blanch the tomatoes in boiling water, remove their skins and seeds.

2. Put the tomatoes on a tray and bake them with the peeled garlic, a little olive oil, the paprika powder and a pinch of pepper for about 20-30 minutes at 180°C.

3. Once removed from the oven, leave for a few minutes to cool a little.

4. Whilst still warm, mix and blend the tomatoes with the grated cheese, stirring until it becomes a smooth paste.

5. Let the almogrote sauce cool and serve as a tapa with bread or toast, or with potato croquettes.

ARRANQUE ROTEÑO (CÁDIZ)

Tomato Gazpacho of Rota (Cádiz)

Rota is a sea port on the coast of Cádiz, famous for its sea foods, but also for a well- known type of gazpacho called "Arranque". The Rota variant is a cousin of the famous gazpacho from Córdoba called "Salmorejo", but with the addition of peppers, an ingredient that makes it different and very tasty. It is a popular local tapa. Here we describe the traditional method of making this dish, using a mortar and pestle to create the "majaillo" - a thick paste used as a base in many soups, sauces and gazpachos in Spain. You can, of course, also use a blender to save time.

Ingredients:

> 1 kg of ripe tomatoes
> 2 peppers (frying or so-called "Italian" peppers)
> 2 medium-sized garlic cloves
> Old bread
> 150 ml of olive oil (approx.)
> Salt

Preparation:

1. Grind all the ingredients together in a large mortar and pestle starting with the garlic, peppers and salt.

2. Add the peeled, chopped tomatoes to the mortar, and gradually add the olive oil until it is all fully incorporated in the paste.

3. Add the breadcrumbs and continue grinding and mixing until the texture is thick and creamy.

4. Serve the "Arranque" in small bowls with slices of bread and pieces of pepper and onion that can be used as a sort of 'spoon'.

CACHORREÑAS DE MÁLAGA

Cachorreña of Málaga

Here is a very minimalist version of an orange soup, often served during hard times or religious fast days.

Ingredients:

> Olive oil
> Salt
> Orange peel
> Ground pepper
> Breadcrumbs
> 1 clove of garlic

Preparation:

1. Put a saucepan of water to boil and add the orange skin and salt.

2. In a mortar, crush the garlic, add the breadcrumbs and gradually add some olive oil and water, mashing all the while to make the paste.

3. When the majado has the required consistency (something like a mayonnaise), add the previously boiled water with orange.

4. Put all this back in the pan on low heat (it should not boil).

5. If you want the soup to have a stronger orange flavour, then add a piece of boiled orange peel in the mortar when grinding the ingredients.

6. Serve with pieces of bread.

CHAMPIÑONES A LA CREMA

Creamed Mushrooms

Ingredients:

> 250 g of fresh mushrooms
> 200 ml of water
> 20 g of butter
> Juice of 1 lemon
> 100 ml of béchamel sauce
> 50 g of cream
> Nutmeg (grated)
> Salt

Preparation:

1. Clean the mushrooms; peel them if they are not very tender.

2. Heat the water with the butter, the lemon juice and a little salt in a saucepan.

3. When this comes to the boil, add the mushrooms. Cover the pan and leave it on the heat for 3 minutes. Remove from the heat and drain well.

4. Warm the béchamel sauce together with the cream and a little salt and nutmeg in a frying pan and mix well.

5. Add the mushrooms, cover the pan and leave the mixture to simmer for two minutes.

6. Serve hot in small dishes with croutons or a small piece of toast.

CREMA DE CALABAZA

Cream of Pumpkin

This rich and nourishing cream can be served as a refreshing cold tapa in the summer, or eaten hot in the cold winter months.

Ingredients:

> Pumpkin
> 1 potato
> Vegetable broth
> Olive oil
> Salt to taste
> Ground black pepper
> Toasted pumpkin seeds

Preparation:

1. Peel and dice a piece of pumpkin and the potato.

2. Boil the pumpkin and potato in a saucepan with some vegetable broth, enough for the pieces to not be completely covered. Add a pinch of pepper, salt, and a little olive oil.

3. Simmer for a few minutes until everything is soft.

4. Blend the cooked mixture until it has the consistency of a soft cream. To make it creamier, you can add a splash of milk.

5. Add more salt to taste.

6. Serve it cold or hot, with a few toasted pumpkin seeds for garnish.

CREMA DE CALABAZA CON ESPECIAS

Cream of Pumpkin with Spices

This is a very tasty autumnal cream soup, sometimes served as a small hot tapa.

Ingredients:

> 1 kg of pumpkin, peeled and diced in small cubes
> 1 leek
> 1 tablespoon of butter
> Salt and black pepper
> Olive oil
> Nutmeg (and/or curry to taste)
> 2 tablespoons of cream

Preparation:

1. Clean and finely chop the leek. Melt the butter in a saucepan and stir in the leek.

2. After a couple of minutes add the diced pumpkin.

3. Partly cover the mixture with water, but not too much or else the result will be too watery.

4. Leave the pan on a low heat for about 20 minutes.

5. When the pumpkin is tender (check with a fork), remove from the heat.

6. Add a little olive oil and two tablespoons of cream. Add the spices (a pinch of nutmeg and a teaspoon of curry powder, if desired).

7. Blend this mixture until it is perfectly smooth. You may adjust the consistency by adding a little water or vegetable stock.

8. Serve hot in a small bowl with a piece of bread, bread sticks or a piece of toast.

CREMA DE CALABACÍN

Cream of Courgette

This is a very easy recipe for a rich, tasty, hot "cream of courgette". It is a perfect warming tapa to serve in the cold months of winter.

Ingredients:

> 2 courgettes
> 1 large potato
> 1 onion
> Milk (optional)
> Olive oil
> Nutmeg
> Salt and pepper

Preparation:

1. Peel, wash and dice the potatoes. Chop the onions. Wash and cut the courgettes into chunks.

2. Sauté the potatoes, onions and courgettes in a little oil.

3. Add the nutmeg, salt and pepper and some water (without covering completely) and place over a high heat until it starts to boil.

4. Cover with a lid and let it simmer on a medium heat until everything is cooked and tender.

5. Blend the mixture, adding a little milk to give it a creamier texture.

6. Serve hot in a small bowl with some croutons or some pieces of fried or toasted bread.

CREMA DE HABAS (BYESSAR)

Cream of Broad Beans (Byessar)

This is a dish that has a Moroccan, Spanish and even a Mexican version. It is known as Byessar or Bissara in Morocco and is very popular. Broad beans are also a very popular vegetable in Spain and every farm will grow some 'habas' for the kitchen. They are often dried and stored for later use. This cream should have the consistency of a dip and is usually eaten cold as a tapa with bread or carrot sticks, or with a tosta.

Ingredients:

400 g of cooked broad beans
2 cloves of garlic
1 onion
100 ml of olive oil
1 teaspoon of ground cumin (or Ras el Hanout - a Moroccan spice mix)
Juice of half a lemon
1 teaspoon of fresh or dried thyme, marjoram, oregano or fresh mint
Salt and black pepper (to taste)
A little water if you want to make the purée a bit lighter

Preparation:

1. If using pre-cooked beans, rinse them first, otherwise cook the fresh broad beans until tender.

2. Gently fry the finely chopped garlic and onion in some olive oil until soft and transparent. Add the beans and let them simmer for about 3-4 minutes.

3. Transfer all the ingredients to a blender. Add the lemon juice, the chosen herbs and spices, olive oil and salt and pepper. Blend the mixture until it has the consistency of a heavy cream. If you prefer, you can lighten the texture with a little water.

4. Let the mix cool and store it in the fridge. Serve the cream with a little mint or sprinkled paprika, a drop of olive oil and some bread or toast.

CREMA FRÍA DE PATATAS Y PUERROS

Cold Leak and Potato Soup

There is a cold leak soup from France called Vichyssoise. However, its origin is unclear. It first began to appear in French recipe books shortly after the return of the Napoleonic armies from Spain. It bears a striking resemblance to traditional recipes that were recorded in the monasteries of Alcantara and Guadalupe and stolen during the Napoleonic invasion. Nonetheless, the recipe of cold leak soup is now popular in both countries and is often served as a cold summer tapa in parts of Spain.

Ingredients:

> 4 leeks
> 2 potatoes
> 1 onion
> 250 ml of cream
> Olive oil
> Salt and pepper

Preparation:

1. Finely chop the onion. Peel, wash and dice the potatoes. Slice the leeks (using only the white parts of the leeks for the soup).

2. Fry the onions in the olive oil until they are transparent.

3. Add the diced potatoes and the leeks to the pan and fry them along with the onion for about 4 minutes, stirring constantly.

4. Add water to the pan to just cover the ingredients. Leave everything to cook together for about 15 minutes.

5. Remove the pan from the heat and season the mixture with salt and pepper. Add the cream and blend the mixture until it has a smooth texture.

6. Allow the soup to cool completely in the refrigerator.

7. Serve in a small bowl with a piece of bread or toast and garnish with a sprig of parsley.

CREMA DE PEPINO Y YOGUR A LA MENTA
Creamed Cucumber and Mint Gazpacho

Although tomato gazpacho is traditionally the main cold soup served in summer in Spain, there are actually several other delicious raw gazpachos, sometimes served as a tapa. Here is the smooth aromatic cream of cucumber and mint gazpacho.

Ingredients:

> 6 cucumbers, ca. 1.5 kg
> 1 cucumber for garnish
> Sesame seeds for garnish
> Juice of 2-3 small lemons
> 4 cloves of garlic
> 10 fresh mint leaves
> 700 ml (approx.) of natural yoghurt
> 50 ml of olive oil
> Salt and pepper

Preparation:

1. Peel and chop the cucumbers and garlic. Chop the mint leaves.

2. Blend the cucumber, lemon juice, yoghurt, chopped mint leaves, garlic and olive oil thoroughly.

3. Add salt and pepper to taste and put the gazpacho in the refrigerator to cool.

4. Serve in small bowls with diced cucumber, sesame seeds and (optionally) ice cubes.

GAZPACHO ANDALUZ

Gazpacho of Andalucía

Gazpacho is a very common dish in Andalucía. It has multiple variants, so we give you several recipes here. There are many more. For example, the onion may be substituted for spring onions. There is also a version called "Chambao", in which we do not blend the ingredients together (as described in this recipe), but just cut them up into very small pieces, put them into a large bowl, mix together with plenty of water and a lot of vinegar, oil, salt and bread and then serve. You may even use an avocado or two instead of bread to create yet another, creamier, gazpacho variant.

One of the main considerations in making gazpacho is that the tomatoes should be ripe, large and juicy. There is a whole range of summer tomatoes available in Andalucía which are suitable - but the main thing is that they should be picked ripe or over-ripe for use in a gazpacho. Shops often keep aside over-ripe tomatoes for the purpose of selling them to customers making gazpacho.

Ingredients:

> 2 large "salad" tomatoes
> 1 green pepper
> 1 medium-sized onion
> 1 cucumber
> Salt
> Olive oil
> Vinegar

Preparation:

1. Chop up the tomatoes, pepper, onion and cucumber.

2. Add the salt, oil and vinegar and blend the mixture well.

3. Finally add cold water, mix well and serve in glasses, garnished with a little finely chopped cucumber and red pepper.

4. It is often served with apple slices, cucumber sticks, grapes or bread.

GAZPACHO DE LOS TRES GOLPES DE MÁLAGA
Gazpacho of "Three Strikes" of Málaga

This is a considered to be one of the most traditional gazpacho recipes in Málaga province in Andalucía. It is simple to make and offers a quick refreshing remedy to combat the summer heat. It is a bit different from other traditional recipes where the ingredients are ground in a mortar and pestle, or blended. This version of gazpacho is made simply by finely chopping the ingredients.

Ingredients:

> 1 kg of ripe tomatoes
> 3 green peppers
> 2 cloves of garlic
> 1 slice of cateto bread (from the previous day)
> 1 onion
> 1 small cucumber
> Fresh garden mint
> Olive oil
> Sherry vinegar
> Salt

Preparation:

1. With a very sharp knife, very finely chop all ingredients and put them into a bowl.

2. Add a splash of olive oil and mix well.

3. Add the "three strikes": vinegar, water and salt, until it is seasoned to your liking.

4. Finally, serve it well-chilled in earthenware or glass bowls.

GAZPACHOS DE ESPARRAGOS TRIGUEROS

Asparagus Gazpacho

Wild asparagus is a real delicacy, and can be found by the side of the roads, the streams and in the hills of the Andalucían countryside. It is a real culinary treasure, as well as being an excellent source of vitamins and minerals and a natural diuretic. Its slightly bitter flavour gives a touch of character to any dish in which it is used, such as omelettes, stir-fries, soups, stews, sauces and this particular gazpacho. Nowadays we can enjoy this dish at any time of the year with cultivated green asparagus, which are less bitter and thicker.

Ingredients:

0.25 kg of wild asparagus
3 hard-boiled eggs
1 litre of water (approx.)
Vinegar (to taste)
Olive oil
Pine nuts or chopped almonds to garnish
Salt (to taste)

Preparation:

1. Chop the asparagus into tiny pieces and bring them to the boil. Cook them until they are soft.

2. Separate the egg whites from the yolks. Put the yolks into a bowl with some salt and a generous splash of oil and mash them until they form a smooth paste. Chop the egg whites.

3. Finally, put the asparagus in a serving bowl, with the chopped egg whites, the egg yolk paste and the cold water. Add vinegar and salt to taste.

GAZPACHO DE ESPÁRRAGOS
Green Asparagus Gazpacho

Gazpacho is a chilled soup, normally made from tomatoes and very traditional to the hot South of Spain, where it is served as a starter or as a tapa served in a glass or small bowl. However, chilled soups can also be made from all kinds of other fresh vegetables. This version of gazpacho uses asparagus and cucumber to produce a very tasty and refreshing tapa.

Ingredients:

> 500 g of green asparagus (wild asparagus, if possible)
> 100 g of stale white bread, diced
> 4 tablespoons of olive oil, plus extra to drizzle
> 3 tablespoons of sherry vinegar or wine vinegar
> 1 cucumber, peeled and deseeded
> Fresh mint to garnish
> 1 teaspoon of salt
> 2 garlic cloves

Preparation:

1. Bring 1 litre of water to the boil and add 1 teaspoon of salt. Meanwhile, cut the asparagus in half, separating the stalks and spears. Cook the spears for 1.5 minutes, until just tender. Lift them out with a slotted spoon, drain and rinse under cold water. Set aside.

2. Bring the water to a simmer and cook the stalks gently for 10 minutes, until very tender. Remove from the heat and cool in the cooking liquid.

3. Put the bread into a bowl with the oil and vinegar. Add half of the cooking liquid and leave to stand for 5 minutes. Dice the cucumber and garlic and add them to the bowl.

4. Put the rest of the cooking liquid and the asparagus stalks into a blender and blend until it has the consistency of a soup.

5. Add the soaked bread, the cucumber and garlic and blend all together until it has a consistent smooth texture. Season and chill.

6. Divide between glasses or small bowls, add a little oil, an asparagus tip and a sprig of mint each. Serve with a little slice of toast.

GAZPACHO DE LIMÓN DE MÁLAGA

Lemon Gazpacho of Málaga

This is an original and refreshing lemon-based gazpacho from Eastern Málaga province.

Ingredients:

> 2 "Zoque" lemons (thick skin with lots of flesh)
> 2 cloves of garlic
> Breadcrumbs from (stale) cateto bread
> 3 tablespoons of olive oil
> 1 teaspoon of paprika powder
> Sherry vinegar
> Salt
> Pepper
> Very cold water

Preparation:

1. Make a "majaillo" in the mortar and pestle with garlic, salt, pepper, paprika and the old bread (soaked in water and then drained).

2. Blend the mixture until it becomes a smooth paste.

3. Gradually add the olive oil to the paste, continuing the blending.

4. Peel the lemon, finely chop it and put it in a bowl. Add the mix and then add a splash of vinegar and some very cold water.

5. Season with salt and vinegar to your taste and serve it very cold.

GAZPACHO DE NERJA

Gazpacho from Nerja

Ingredients:

     1.5 kg of ripe tomatoes (peeled)
     Half an onion
     1 small cucumber
     1 small green pepper
     250 g of breadcrumbs (from the day before) soaked in water
     Olive oil
     Vinegar
     Salt
     1.5 litre of very cold water
     2 garlic cloves

Preparation:

1. Peel the tomatoes and remove the seeds.

2. Blend all vegetables together: tomatoes, sliced onion, peeled cucumber and pepper, along with salt, vinegar, oil and breadcrumbs. If the mixture is too thick, add some water.

3. When everything is well blended, add the remaining water and blend again slowly to make sure that all the ingredients are fully mixed. When it has reached the desired consistency, pour the gazpacho into bowls ready for serving.

4. You can accompany the gazpacho with some finely chopped onion, cucumber and pepper, served in a separate bowl so that everyone can add what they like to their own gazpacho.

GAZPACHO DE PEPINO Y AGUACATE

Gazpacho of Cucumber and Avocado

This is another cold creamy gazpacho served as a summertime tapa, this time made with avocado and cucumber. It is easy and quick to prepare and produces an exquisite result.

It is important to use fully ripened avocados for this dish. When buying avocados for use the same day, check to see if they are ripe by pressing the fruit lightly to see if the flesh gives a little.

Ingredients:

>3 ripe avocados
>3 cucumbers
>2 cloves of garlic
>6 tablespoons of olive oil
>A little natural yoghurt (optional)
>Juice of 1.5 lemons
>Fresh dill to decorate
>Salt and pepper

Preparation:

1. Peel the cucumbers and chop them into a blender bowl.

2. Cut the avocados in half lengthwise, remove the stone and add the flesh to the chopped cucumbers.

3. Peel and roughly chop the garlic and add them to the bowl.

4. Add the olive oil and lemon juice (avoid adding pips, because they'll make the soup bitter).

5. Add salt and pepper to taste.

6. Blend all the ingredients into a smooth and consistent cream. You can blend in a little yoghurt at this point if you wish to make the soup creamier.

7. Place the soup in the refrigerator to cool.

8. Serve the gazpacho decorated with diced avocado, cucumber and onion, sprinkled with a little pepper and garnished with a sprig of dill.

GAZPACHUELO DE ANDALUCÍA

Gazpachuelo of Andalucía

Ingredients:

> 2 eggs
> 0.25 litres of olive oil
> Salt
> Vinegar or lemon juice
> Bread

Preparation:

1. Put 1 egg in a blender and slowly blend in the olive oil to form a smooth mayonnaise, add salt and vinegar (or lemon juice). Add water to get the consistency you prefer.

2. Put some water in a pan and bring to the boil. Break the second egg into the boiling water.

3. When it starts foaming, remove the pan from the heat and very carefully stir in the mayonnaise, taking care to avoid any lumps, until it becomes a white broth.

4. Try it and, if necessary, add salt and vinegar.

5. Serve hot in a bowl with pieces of bread.

MOJO PICÓN

Piquant Mojo

Here is one of several mojo recipes, this time using the hot red pepper called "pimienta picona" from the Islas Canarias. This may not be readily available, so this recipe suggests using cayenne pepper or any other hot pepper.

Ingredients:

> 1 head of garlic (about 8 cloves)
> 2 picona peppers (or 2 cayenne or other hot peppers)
> 1 teaspoon of cumin seeds
> 1 teaspoon of paprika powder
> 1 tablespoon of wine vinegar
> 15 tablespoons of olive oil
> 1 level teaspoon of salt

Preparation:

1. Mojo is traditionally made by grinding the ingredients slowly together with a mortar and pestle whilst gradually adding oil and vinegar. A faster way of making the mojo is simply to put all the ingredients together in a blender and blend them until you have a sauce of a quite thick consistency - like a dip.

2. If needed, you can make the mojo a little thinner with some water.

3. When it is ready, store it in the fridge until serving.

4. Mojos are served with a variety of dishes - especially with the Canary "wrinkled potatoes", but also make a delicious tapa as a spread or dip with bread or toast.

MOJO VERDE CANARIO DE CILANTRO

Green Mojo of the Canaries

Mojos are a traditional, tasty and easy to make sauce of the Islas Canarias. This recipe is for a green mojo. It can be prepared with parsley instead of coriander or with a mix of both herbs. You can also add 2 or 3 green Canary peppers.

Ingredients:

>1 head of garlic (8-10 cloves)
>1 bunch of cilantro
>1 teaspoon of cumin seeds
>2 tablespoons of vinegar
>15 tablespoons of olive oil
>1 teaspoon of coarse salt

Preparation:

1. Mojo is traditionally made by grinding the ingredients slowly together with a mortar and pestle whilst gradually adding oil and vinegar. A faster method is simply to put all the ingredients together in a blender and blend them until you have a smooth paste.

2. If the mojo is too thick, add some water.

3. Mojos are served with a variety of tapas - especially with the Canary "wrinkled potatoes" - but also make a mouth-watering tapa spread on a simple slice of bread or with a little slice of cheese.

PASTILLAS DE CALDO DE VERDURAS

Vegetable Stock Cubes

Making your own vegetable stock cubes is not very traditional, but if you are a vegetarian, it's quite essential. Vegetable stock is used in many recipes. It's a good alternative to the commercial products, and making them yourself also allows you to control your own salt and fat intake.

Ingredients:

> 1 litre of water
> 20 g of olive oil
> 1 teaspoon of coarse salt
> 2 or 3 cloves
> A few black pepper corns
> 0.5 teaspoon of turmeric
> 0.5 teaspoon of ginger
> 1 bay leaf
> 2 cloves of garlic
> 1 carrot
> 1 stick of celery
> 1 leek
> 1 onion

Preparation

1. Peel and wash the vegetables. Cut them into large pieces.

2. Boil all the ingredients in the water and simmer for about 30 minutes or until tender.

3. Drain, and blend the vegetables.

4. Prepare an ice-cube tray by coating it with plastic cling film.

5. Pour the blended vegetables into the ice-cube trays, cover them with foil and allow the mix to cool. When cool, place the containers in the freezer. When the cubes are frozen, remove them from the moulds and store them in the freezer in bags until needed.

PORRA DE MÁLAGA
Cold Soup with Egg and Broad Beans of Málaga

A "porra" is like a gazpacho, but thicker. Here is a generic recipe from the province of Málaga (also called Porra Antequerana because of its popularity around the old town of Antequera); you can vary the quantity of the ingredients according to taste.

Ingredients:

> 4 ripe tomatoes
> 1 pepper
> 1 clove of garlic
> Breadcrumbs (cateto bread)
> Olive oil
> Vinegar
> Salt

To add:

> Broad beans
> 1 egg

Preparation:

1. Put the ingredients in a blender and blend until you have the consistency of a thick gazpacho. Pass them through a purée mill.

2. When the porra is ready, serve it in a small bowl alone or with chopped hardboiled eggs and broad beans (cooked).

PURÉ DE CALABAZA

Pumpkin Purée

This is a simple recipe for a tasty pumpkin purée with a touch of ginger and cumin. It is very easy to prepare and ideal as a hot starter or a tapa.

Ingredients:

> 1 kg of peeled, cleaned pumpkin
> 2 leeks, chopped in slices
> 1 clove of garlic, crushed
> 3 tablespoons of olive oil
> 1 teaspoon of ground cumin
> 1 teaspoon of ground ginger
> 1 litre of vegetable stock
> Salt and pepper

Preparation:

1. Cut the peeled pumpkin into small pieces.

2. Fry the crushed garlic and sliced leeks with the olive oil in a large pan over a low heat. When everything is tender, add the cumin and ginger and stir for a minute.

3. Now add the pumpkin and season to taste.

4. Add the vegetable stock and increase the heat. Leave to boil until the pumpkin is cooked (about 30 minutes).

5. Mash or blend until obtaining the desired consistency. Add a little water or stock if you like the mix to be thinner. It can be anywhere from a thick purée to a light cream.

6. Serve hot with some little pieces of toast.

PURÉ DE PUERROS

Leek Purée

This is a simple and very tasty recipe for a leek purée. Leeks always give dishes an intense flavour, which makes for a delicious tapa.

Ingredients:

> 1 kilo of leeks
> 1 onion
> 3 large potatoes
> Olive oil
> Pepper
> Salt
> Butter

Preparation:

1. Chop up the onion and fry it in some olive oil in a large pan until tender.

2. Meanwhile, clean and slice the potatoes and the leeks. When the onion is "transparent", add the leeks and potatoes. Fry together for a couple of minutes.

3. After that, just cover the vegetables with water. Add a teaspoon of salt (or to your taste). Cover the pan and bring it to the boil. Leave it to simmer until all the ingredients are tender.

4. Season with a little pepper and add a tablespoon of butter.

5. Blend the mixture until well puréed. Adjust the seasoning if necessary and serve in a small bowl with a drop of olive oil and some toast or croutons.

PURÉ DE ZANAHORIA

Carrot Purée

Ingredients:

3 carrots
1 small onion
1 potato
Olive oil
Salt

Preparation:

1. Wash, peel and chop all of the vegetables.

2. Boil all the vegetables together in a saucepan until tender.

3. Drain the vegetables and blend them all together until obtaining a smooth purée.

4. If you prefer the purée to be creamier, add in a little of the cooking water during blending.

5. Serve with a splash of olive oil, hot in small bowls or cold in a glass. Serve alone or with some toasted bread or croutons.

SALMOREJO DE CÓRDOBA
Salmorejo - Cold Soup of Córdoba

Salmorejo is a type of gazpacho (cold soup), quite similar to the thicker porra. It comes from western Andalucía and is most traditional in the province of Córdoba. It is commonly served as a tapa and, like porra, is traditionally accompanied by chopped, hard-boiled egg. There are many variations of salmorejo, including some served with ham, so when ordering it in a bar, be sure to ask for it without ham!

Ingredients:

> 2 eggs
> Stale bread in crumbs
> 2 large cloves of garlic (or more, to taste)
> 1 kg of ripe tomatoes
> 250 ml of olive oil
> 60 ml of red wine vinegar
> Salt to taste

Preparation:

1. Hard-boil the eggs. Place them in ice-cold water to cool. Refrigerate until ready to serve.

2. Cut the bread into slices of about 1 cm thick. Pour about 0.5 cm water into a large dish. Add the bread slices and allow the bread to soak up the water for 30 minutes. Squeeze excess water out of the slices and place them in a blender.

3. Peel and dice the garlic and add them to the bread in the blender. Peel and deseed the tomatoes. Add to the blender and pour in the vinegar. Blend the mixture.

4. Gradually add the olive oil while blending. Continue adding the oil until the mixture is smooth. If it is too thick, add a little cold water while blending.

5. The salmorejo should have the consistency of soft mayonnaise.

6. Serve chilled in a small bowl or glass with a drop of olive oil and a piece of bread or toast. If you wish, chop some of the hardboiled egg and sprinkle a little on top.

SALSA DE AJO CON ACEITUNAS

Garlic Sauce with Olives

Ingredients:

>500 ml of olive oil
>100 g of pickled capers
>30 g of green olives
>Salt and black pepper
>Half a head of garlic
>4 raw egg yolks
>Lemon juice

Preparation:

1. Peel the garlic cloves and then grind them in a blender with a little salt.

2. Remove the stone from the olives and add to the mix. Drain the capers and add them also to the blender.

3. Blend all of the ingredients with enough olive oil to obtain a creamy paste.

4. Add the egg yolks and continue to blend until everything is well mixed.

5. Season and add lemon juice to your taste.

6. The sauce can be kept in the refrigerator for 3-4 days.

SALSA ROMESCO
Romesco Sauce

Romesco sauce originates in Tarragona, in North-eastern Spain. It is said that it was originally made by the fishermen of the area, but it is also a tasty sauce to accompany vegetables. It is very popular in Spain and is even used in some olive marinades. As a tapa it is lovely by itself, simply spread on a slice of country bread, or eaten with a bread stick or a small slice of toast.

Ingredients:

    12 blanched almonds
    10-12 hazelnuts
    1 head of garlic
    1 slice of stale bread
    1 large ripe tomato
    2 large roasted red peppers (known as ñoras)
    230 ml of olive oil (approx.)
    110 ml of red wine or sherry vinegar
    1 small hot pepper

Preparation:

1. Rub off excess dry skin from the garlic head. Then place the garlic on a baking tray and pour a bit of olive oil on top. Roast the garlic in the oven at 150°C for about 20 minutes - or until the garlic is soft on the inside.

2. Put the almonds and hazelnuts into a blender and blend until they are finely ground.

3. Quickly fry the bread in a little olive oil until both sides are browned. Remove the bread from the pan and allow to cool on a paper towel.

4. Cut the tomatoes into quarters and sauté these in a frying pan with a little oil for 4 to 5 minutes. Remove the pan from the heat.

5. Once the bread has cooled, tear it into pieces and blend it together with the nuts in the blender. Add the sautéed tomatoes and continue to blend. Squeeze the roasted garlic from the skins into the processor. Add the roasted red peppers to the blender with the other ingredients and continue to blend the ingredients until obtaining a thick purée.

6. Whilst blending, gradually add the oil and vinegar. Add salt to taste. When the correct consistency is achieved, cool the mixture in the refrigerator.

7. Serve as a tapa with a slice of bread or use with other tapas recipes.

8. The sauce can be stored chilled for up to 7 days.

SOPA DE ESPÁRRAGOS DE MÁLAGA

Asparagus Soup of Málaga

Ingredients:

> Asparagus
> Onion
> Garlic
> Almonds
> Bread
> Eggs
> Salt
> Lemon
> Saffron

Preparation:

1. Make the majado: Put a little oil in a frying pan, fry the almonds, a clove of garlic and a slice of bread. Then grind them in a mortar with some strands of saffron and a little salt.

2. Fry the chopped onion in the same oil until tender, add the chopped asparagus and mix together with the onion.

3. In the meantime, put some water in a saucepan (amount depends on how thick you like the soup) and bring to the boil. When the water starts to boil add the asparagus and onions mix.

4. After about half an hour, add the majado, simmer for a few minutes, then remove from the heat.

5. Whisk an egg yolk with the juice of half a lemon and carefully, so as not to break up the egg mix, pour it into the soup, and serve.

SOPA DE ESPÁRRAGOS DE PERIANA

Asparagus Soup of Periana in Málaga

Ingredients:

> 2 ripe tomatoes
> 2 green peppers
> 1 onion
> 3 cloves of garlic
> 250 g of asparagus
> 100 g of almonds
> A slice of fried bread
> 1 roasted red pepper
> A sprig of mint
> Salt
> Olive oil
> Pepper

Preparation:

1. Make the majado: Fry the almonds, bread and garlic in olive oil, and then grind the mixture in a mortar.

2. Make the sofrito sauce with the tomato, the green peppers and onion.

3. Wash and chop up the asparagus. Put water into a saucepan for the soup and heat. The amount of water depends on how thick the final soup should be.

4. Add the sofrito and majado, the chopped asparagus, and the roasted pepper. Season to your taste with salt and pepper.

5. Simmer for 20 minutes. Add a sprig of mint.

6. Serve the soup with fried or toasted bread croutons.

SOPA DE MAIMONES

Garlic Soup "Maimones"

The ideal "partner" for this soup is that firm, traditional type of bread called "cateto" and it needs to be at least three or four days old. In some places, the egg is added to the soup, lightly beaten, giving it a characteristic appearance.

Ingredients:

> Several slices of hard cateto bread
> 1 head of garlic
> 1 ripe tomato, peeled
> Olive oil
> Salt
> One egg per plate
> 1.5 litre of water

Preparation:

1. Brown the garlic and the finely chopped tomato with a little salt over a medium heat in a frying pan with a drop of olive oil.

2. When they are fried, add a litre and a half of water and boil over a high heat.

3. Place a thin slice of the cateto bread on each plate. Poach the eggs in the soup (keeping it hot without allowing it to boil), and when poached, add one egg to each plate, along with the soup.

SOPA FRÍA DE PEPINO

Cold Cucumber Soup

Here is a cold soup which is easy to make and, like gazpacho, is served as a refreshing summer tapa.

Ingredients:

> 2 teaspoons of olive oil
> 5 cucumbers (chopped)
> 3 cloves of garlic
> 2 onions (diced)
> 600 ml of vegetable broth
> 60 ml of chopped fresh dill
> Black pepper to taste
> 250 ml of milk or yogurt

Preparation:

1. Heat the olive oil over a medium heat in a large saucepan and sauté the cucumbers, the garlic and onion until the onion is transparent (about 6 minutes).

2. Add the vegetable broth and cook over a low heat until the cucumber is tender (15 to 20 minutes).

3. Remove the soup from the heat and blend it until it is smooth. Before the soup cools, add the dill and season with pepper to taste.

4. Chill the soup. Add 250 ml of milk or yogurt before serving.

SOPA DE TOMATE DE MÁLAGA

Tomato Soup from Málaga

Ingredients:

> 2 green peppers
> 3 ripe tomatoes
> 1 onion
> Cumin (to taste)
> Saffron (to taste)
> A dash of lemon juice or vinegar
> Bread
> 350 g almonds
> 1 clove of garlic

Preparation:

1. Chop the tomatoes, peppers and onions as finely as possible.

2. Crush the garlic.

3. Fry the crushed garlic with the almonds until golden. Slightly toast the almonds but don't allow them to become too dark. Sprinkle some cumin on top. Put aside without allowing it to cool.

4. Put some water in a saucepan and bring to the boil. There should be enough water to cover the tomatoes, peppers and onions by about 3 cm. As soon as the water is boiling, add the tomatoes, peppers and onions as well as the garlic and almond mix. Simmer for 20 -30 minutes (or until all ingredients are tender).

5. Fry some bread in the frying pan with the olive oil to accompany the soup - it should be well toasted, but not burnt.

6. Finally, add a little lemon juice (or vinegar) to the soup (to taste) before serving.

SOPA DE TRIGUEROS

Asparagus Soup

Ideally we would suggest that you go out into the mountains of Andalucía and gather wild asparagus for this recipe. Once upon a time this precious delicacy was just a subsistence food for the poor. Now, of course, you can buy commercially grown asparagus in any supermarket for many months of the year. But they do not taste the same. Wild asparagus are bright green and quite thin unlike the cultivated green asparagus which has a rather fleshy stem. The season for wild asparagus is short and they are at their best at the beginning of the season. The popular proverb says of the coveted green asparagus: "In April they are for me, in May they are for my horse and in June they are for no-one."

Ingredients :

> 350 g of asparagus
> 2 tomatoes
> 2 peppers
> 1 onion
> 1 egg per person
> 4 or 5 cloves of garlic
> Half a teaspoon of paprika powder
> 1 sprig of parsley
> Black pepper (to taste)
> 1 slice of cateto bread (150 g)
> 1.5 litre of water (approx.)
> Saffron
> Olive oil
> Salt (to taste)

Preparation:

1. Wash the spears of asparagus, chop them up as small as possible and put aside.

2. Make a sofrito with 2 cloves of garlic, peppers, onions and tomatoes and, when half cooked, add the chopped asparagus, let it finish and then set aside.

3. Make a majado: in a frying pan with olive oil, fry the chopped up remaining garlic cloves with the bread and, once golden, put it in a mortar with pepper and paprika powder, and grind the mixture.

4. Bring the water to the boil in a pan and when it's boiling add the sofrito mix, saffron and the majado paste with some salt to season. Simmer for 15-20 minutes.

5. When it is ready to be removed from the heat, add the eggs to poach. Chop them up and let them boil again for a short moment.

6. Depending on the area and on your preference, you can add fried bread croutons to the soup; sometimes people add cumin seeds or some fried almonds to the majado, or you can beat the eggs before adding them to the pan, making sure the soup is not boiling, to prevent the eggs from being broken up.

7. Vinegar is often added on the plate, according to your taste.

SORBETE DE AGUACATE

Avocado Sorbet

This is a refreshing sorbet tapa made with avocados. There are many variations on this recipe, some using yoghurt and nuts. Avocados are very suitable for both sweet and savoury sorbets.

Ingredients:

> 2 avocados
> 1 clove of garlic
> Lemon juice
> 400 ml vegetable stock (see recipe for vegetable stock)
> Salt

Preparation:

1. Cut the avocados into 2 halves. Remove the stone and take out the pulp. You can keep the skins to serve the sorbet in, if you wish.

2. Blend the avocado pulp with the garlic and the vegetable stock. Add salt and lemon juice and mix all ingredients together well.

3. Place the mixture in the freezer.

4. Just before the mixture hardens blend it to avoid ice crystals forming, and freeze it again.

5. When it has achieved the required consistency, serve the sorbet in glasses or in the avocado skins.

SORBETE DE PEPINO

Cucumber Sorbet

A refreshing savoury cucumber sorbet served as an appetiser in the hot summer months.

Ingredients:

> 1 medium-sized cucumber
> The juice of 1 lemon
> 220 ml of cream
> Iced water
> Salt (to taste)
> Pepper (to taste)
> Slices of lemon and/or cucumber and a few mint leaves - to decorate

Preparation:

1. Peel and chop the cucumber. Mix with enough lemon juice, cream and water to obtain the density of a thick purée. Season the mixture to your taste with salt and pepper.

2. Place the mix in the freezer until it has the consistency of a sorbet. Put it into individual glasses and serve, garnished with slices of lemon and/or cucumber and mint.

SORBETE DE PEPINO A LA MENTA

Cucumber Sorbet with Mint

This is another variation on savoury cucumber sorbet.

Ingredients:

>2 cucumbers
>200 ml of natural yogurt
>Chopped fresh mint (to taste)
>Freshly ground pepper
>10 tablespoons of vegetable stock (see recipe in this book)

Preparation:

1. Cut the cucumbers in half lengthwise. Carefully remove and mash up the cucumber pulp. Keep the cucumber "boats" for serving the sorbet.

2. Mix the cucumber pulp and yogurt together with the chopped fresh mint, a pinch of pepper and the vegetable stock.

3. Put the mixture in the freezer.

4. Before the mixture hardens, blend it and fill up the "cucumber boats". Garnish with some fresh mint and serve at once.

VEGANESA (MAYONESA VEGETAL)

Mayonnaise without Eggs

Whilst this is not strictly a traditional recipe, we decided to include a recipe for a mayonnaise substitute which did not use eggs. Mayonnaise is such a popular sauce and so often used in tapas recipes, that we felt it would be useful to provide an egg-free recipe alternative for vegans, thus opening up many excellent recipes which would otherwise be missed.

There are many "veganesa" recipes, but here we give one which is a really good substitute. The use of soy milk is really a necessity because it is rich in lecithin - a powerful emulsifier - and a substitute for eggs to allow for the oil and water to mix successfully. It's a slightly complicated recipe, but worth the trouble.

Ingredients:

> 120 ml of unsweetened soy milk
> 2 teaspoons of tapioca starch
> 6 tablespoons of grape seed oil or light olive oil
> 4 g of corn powder
> 1.5 tablespoons of apple cider vinegar
> 1 teaspoon of salt
> A pinch of paprika

Preparation:

1. Put all the ingredients into a blender or small food processor and blend until smooth and the oil has been mixed well with the soy milk.

2. Make a double boiler: Put a stainless steel bowl that rests on the lip of a small sauce pan with a lid. Put about 2 cm of water in the bottom of the pan, cover, and bring to a boil.

3. Put the mayonnaise mixture into the bowl. When the water comes to a boil, turn down the heat, remove the lid and carefully place the bowl into the saucepan.

4. Heat, stirring constantly, until the temperature of the mayonnaise is about 65°C. At this point the mayonnaise should have the consistency of real, quite thick mayonnaise. It shouldn't be thin.

5. When the right consistency is achieved, immediately remove the bowl from the double boiler and place it in a cold-water bath to stop the cooking.

6. Store the mayonnaise in an air-tight container in the fridge. You can add in a little mustard to your taste.

ZOQUE

Zoque

"Zoque" is thought by some to be a term derived from the Arabic, meaning "suqât" which means "worthless". It may refer to the old pieces of bread which had become hard and unfit for consumption; hence the definition of "zoquete" by the Royal Academy as: "A piece of bread, thick and irregular, left over from the food and kept in the bag for recycling as breadcrumbs, soup or gazpacho base".

In reality, a zoque is just another variation of gazpacho, but with less formality. As mentioned already, the word 'zoque' is not recorded as an official word by the Royal Academy of Spain, except as a "thick, irregular piece of bread". Perhaps this is the true origin of the name of the dish, given that it is really just some pieces of toasted old bread, together with a tasty paste or thick soup.

There are many variations on the "zoque" theme, ranging from those based on lemon to the tomato version we give below. All of them are a tribute to the ingenuity of the people, not only to create new recipes with very limited resources, but also to cool the summer heat.

Ingredients:

> 1 kg of tomatoes
> 1 pepper
> 1 clove of garlic
> Bread
> 0.5 litre of olive oil
> Vinegar
> Salt

Preparation:

1. Peel and chop the tomatoes, peppers and garlic, add the breadcrumbs with the oil, salt, and vinegar (to taste).

2. Blend everything together. Add water and sieve it through a purée press until it has the correct consistency of a thick, cold soup.

---oOo---

2.6 Potato Tapas

AJOARRIERO

Potato and Garlic Purée

Ajoarriero is a potato purée, typically found in the regions of Aragón, Navarra, Cuenca, Castilla and León, País Vasco and around Requena-Utiel. It is made with potatoes, garlic, egg and olive oil, finely crushed in a mortar. It is often used as an addition to other dishes.

The purée is believed to originate with the muleteers (arrieros), who worked in those days as couriers over long distances and who used the dish as a means of preserving their food on these long and arduous journeys in the summer months. Gradually, the recipe was introduced into the inns and bars where these muleteers stayed overnight. It has since entered into popular food culture.

Today, this purée is considered a great delicacy. It is used in various other dishes including traditional cod recipes, stuffed courgettes, and with pastas like cannelloni. It is also served on toast as a tasty tapa.

Ingredients:

> 500 g of potatoes
> 4 eggs
> 3 cloves of garlic
> 350 ml of olive oil
> Salt

Preparation:

1. Wash the potatoes well, but leave them in the skin.

2. Hard-boil the eggs. Peel the garlic cloves.

3. Boil the potatoes until they are tender.

4. Peel the potatoes and mash them into a purée with a little of their cooking water.

5. Grind the garlic with a little salt and two of the hard-boiled egg yolks in a large mortar.

6. Put the contents of the mortar into a large bowl, then add the mashed potatoes and mix all the ingredients well with a little salt. Gradually add the olive oil to the mix.

7. Chop up the remaining two boiled eggs and add them to the mix.

8. Mix thoroughly and put the purée in the fridge.

9. Serve cold with slices of toast. Ajoarriero is also often served together with other vegetables such as broccoli or cauliflower.

ENSALADILLA DE PATATA
Potato Salad

Ingredients:

>4 medium-sized potatoes
>3 carrots, peeled
>140 ml of peas (fresh cooked or frozen)
>1 teaspoon of salt
>3 tablespoons of olive oil
>2 piquillo (red) peppers, chopped
>1 hard-boiled egg, chopped
>1 spring onion, finely chopped
>3 tablespoons of chopped mixed pickles (onions, gherkins, etc.)
>1 teaspoon of Dijon mustard
>3 tablespoons of chopped fresh parsley
>140 ml of mayonnaise (see the recipe for mayonnaise)
>3 tablespoons of white wine vinegar
>Chives to decorate and Capers, drained

Preparation:

1. Boil the potatoes (unpeeled) and the carrots until tender. Cook the peas until tender. Drain the vegetables and put them into the fridge to cool.

2. Peel the potatoes and cut them in 1 cm cubes. Dice the carrots. Mix the carrots, potatoes and peas together in a bowl. Add the salt, olive oil, chopped piquillo peppers, egg and onion.

3. In a separate bowl, mix the chopped pickles, mustard, chopped parsley, mayonnaise and vinegar. Whisk until smooth.

4. Stir this sauce into the potato mix. Leave this mixture to stand for 2 hours at room temperature or, covered and refrigerated for up to 24 hours.

5. Serve cold or at room temperature in small bowls or spread on bread. Garnish the top with capers and/or fresh chives.

PAPAS ALIÑADAS DE CÁDIZ

Marinated Potatoes of Cádiz

This is a typical tapa of the province of Cádiz. It is also to be found in Sevilla province, but there it is usually eaten as a main course with fried egg. In other parts of Andalucía, this is also eaten with a salmorejo sauce.

Ingredients:

> 1 kg of new potatoes
> 1 or 2 spring onions (depending on size)
> Fresh parsley
> Olive oil
> Vinegar of Jerez
> Coarse salt

Preparation:

1. Cook the potatoes (with skins, but well washed) in salted water.

2. When tender, remove them from the heat and let them stand in the water for half an hour.

3. Drain the potatoes, remove their skin, cut them into thick slices and place them in a bowl.

4. Chop the onions and the parsley and add them to the potatoes. Add the coarse salt, then the vinegar and then the oil. Stir and serve cool.

PATATAS CON AJO Y PEREJIL

Potatoes with Garlic and Parsley

There are many recipes for potatoes with garlic and parsley; this simple version comes from Jaén in Andalucía, a town famous for its generous tapas.

Ingredients:

>900 g of potatoes cut in ½ cm slices
>Olive oil - sufficient to just cover the potatoes in a deep pan
>4 cloves (or more) of garlic, peeled and roughly chopped
>Fresh parsley, chopped
>1 tablespoon of sweet paprika powder
>1-2 tablespoons of white wine vinegar

Preparation:

1. Heat the oil gently and add the potatoes.

2. Allow the potatoes to stew slowly in the oil until cooked. Do not allow them to go brown.

3. Drain off most of the oil, add the garlic and parsley and cook for a further minute or two.

4. At the last moment, stir in the paprika powder and add the white wine vinegar.

5. Do not allow the paprika to cook for too long or it will become bitter.

6. Serve as a tapa with alioli or with some salad and fresh bread.

PATATAS ALIOLI (I)

Fried Potatoes with Garlic Mayonnaise

There are two versions of this popular tapa. One is served fried and hot and the other is served boiled and cold.

Here is the recipe for the hot version.

Ingredients:

> 4-5 medium potatoes
> Olive oil for frying
> Fresh parsley, chopped
> Alioli sauce - Garlic mayonnaise (See the recipe in the chapter "Sauces")

Preparation:

1. Peel the potatoes. Cut them into 1-2 cm blocks. Sprinkle with salt.

2. Pour olive oil into a deep frying pan. Warm the oil on medium heat. When it is hot enough, fry the potatoes.

3. Once the potatoes are fried (after about 10 minutes), remove them from the pan and leave to drain.

4. Place the potatoes in a large bowl. Pour the alioli over the potatoes and toss carefully together with the parsley.

5. Place the potatoes with sauce into small individual bowls. Serve warm.

6. This tapa is often served side by side with patatas bravas.

PATATAS ALIOLI (II)

Potatoes in Garlic Mayonnaise (II)

This is the cold version of patatas alioli. In this recipe the potatoes are boiled, not fried, and then allowed to cool before adding the mayonnaise sauce. This is a universally favourite tapa in Spain.

Ingredients:

15 ml of Dijon mustard
80 ml of mayonnaise
2 garlic cloves, finely chopped
Black pepper to taste
Paprika to taste
1.4 kg of potatoes
60 g of finely chopped onion

Preparation:

1. Peel the potatoes and cut them into cubes of about 3 cm. Boil these until just tender. Do not overcook them; they should remain firm. Leave to cool.

2. Mix the mustard with the mayonnaise, garlic and pepper in a bowl. Add a little paprika powder to taste.

3. Stir the potatoes and onions into the sauce.

4. Refrigerate for at least 1 hour before serving in small bowls, alone or with bread sticks.

PATATAS AL AJILLO

Garlic Potatoes

Ingredients:

750 g of small new potatoes
Sea salt
6 cloves of garlic
1 onion
6 tablespoons of olive oil
A few sprigs of rosemary
1 tablespoon of paprika
Fresh parsley

Preparation:

1. Wash and scrub the potatoes. Boil them in plenty of salty water for about 15-20 minutes and drain them.

2. Peel the onions and garlic and chop them finely. Wash the rosemary, separate the leaves from the stems and chop them finely. Wash and finely chop the parsley.

3. Fry the garlic, onion and rosemary in hot olive oil, stirring occasionally.

4. Add the fried ingredients to the potatoes. Sprinkle with paprika and parsley and put on the heat again. Keep mixing the ingredients until the potatoes are well coated with all the other ingredients.

5. Serve hot in small bowls.

PATATAS AL AJILLO CON TOMATE
Garlic Potatoes with Tomato Sauce

Ingredients:

Potatoes
2 bay leaves
Olive oil
2 cloves of garlic
Cumin seeds
Black pepper
Saffron
Water
Tomato purée
Salt

Preparation:

1. Dice the potatoes into largish chunks.

2. Fry the potatoes in olive oil with bay leaves on a low heat. When they are fried put them aside.

3. Use a mortar and pestle to crush the garlic, the cumin seeds, the pepper and the saffron. Add a little water and the tomato purée and blend everything together well.

4. Remove most of the oil from the frying pan, and then toss the potatoes in the pan, mixing them with the sauce over a low heat.

6. Serve in small bowls.

PAPAS ARRUGADAS CON MOJO PICÓN

Wrinkled Potatoes with Hot Pepper Sauce

Potatoes have been cultivated in the Islas Canarias since the 17th century when they were brought back from the Americas. The people of the Canarias call these potatoes "papas", which is the Native American name, while in the rest of Spain they are usually called "patatas". These "wrinkled potatoes" are a traditional dish, served with a "mojo" or sauce. The "mojo" is made with garlic and peppers, is slightly piquant and very tasty. The two are often served together as a starter, side dish or tapa.

Mojo Picón - Garlic and pepper sauce:

Ingredients:

5 garlic cloves
1 teaspoon of cumin seed
2-3 small dried chilli peppers
Salt
30 g of breadcrumbs
Half a teaspoon of paprika powder
45 ml of red wine vinegar
75 ml of olive oil
140 ml water (or as required)

Preparation:

1. Using a mortar and pestle, grind the cumin, garlic, and chillies with some salt to taste. The mixture should be mashed well.

2. Add the paprika powder, the vinegar and oil, and continue to blend.

3. Add breadcrumbs and mash together.

4. Gradually add water until the sauce has the desired consistency.

5. Pour the mojo over the potatoes and serve.

Ingredients:

1.25 kg of small potatoes
2 tablespoons of coarse sea salt

Preparation:

1. Clean the potatoes and remove "eyes" - do not peel them. Place the potatoes in a large pot and boil them in water with the salt for 15-20 minutes until cooked.

2. Remove from the heat and drain off the water. Put the pot with the potatoes back on the stove, allowing any remaining water to dry off. You should see a layer of salt form on the dry skins, which will then wrinkle.

3. Serve the "papas" with the mojo picón.

PATATAS ASADAS PICANTES

Spicy Roast Potatoes

If you like a more spicy taste, you can add more chilli and pepper and vice versa. These spicy roast potatoes can be served with a variety of sauces such as garlic mayonnaise, yogurt sauce, roasted garlic sauce, mustard sauce and honey, etc., or no sauce at all.

Ingredients:

> 400 grams of potatoes
> A mixture of equal parts of rosemary, thyme, oregano, marjoram, parsley, sage, dried onion, and garlic powder, with black pepper, cayenne powder, mustard seeds and salt added to taste.
> Rice flour
> Olive oil

Preparation:

1. Wash and clean the potatoes but leave the skin. Cut the potatoes into wedges.

2. Mix the herbs and spices and a spoonful of rice flour in a bowl with some salt and olive oil. Stir in the potatoes, making sure that the potatoes are well coated with the mixture.

3. Preheat the oven to 210°C for roasting. Spread the potatoes on a roasting tray and place in the oven for 20 minutes. Spray the potatoes with a little more olive oil and lower the temperature to 180°C.

4. Continue roasting until the potatoes are tender inside and crispy brown on the outside.

5. Before serving, add salt if necessary.

6. Serve hot by themselves or with your chosen sauce.

PATATAS ASADAS CON SALSA DE PIMIENTO DEL PIQUILLO

Roasted Potatoes with Red Pepper Sauce

Ingredients:

For the potatoes and sofrito:

4 medium-sized potatoes
50 g of onion
1 red pepper
1 clove of garlic

For the piquillo pepper sauce:

100 g of red onion
2 cloves of garlic
250 g of roasted piquillo peppers (also good from a jar or tin)
500 ml of homemade tomato sauce
6 tablespoons of olive oil
1-2 teaspoons of sugar
Salt

Preparation:

1. Bake the unpeeled potatoes, wrapped in foil, in the oven at 200°C for 40 minutes.

2. Remove the foil and cut the potatoes into slices.

3. Make a "sofrito" sauce by dicing the onion, garlic and red pepper and cooking these in a frying pan with a few tablespoons of olive oil for a few minutes on a medium heat.

4. Drain the excess oil from the sofrito and pour it over the slices of potato.

6. To prepare the piquillo pepper sauce: Sauté the sliced garlic and onion in a hot pan with olive oil. Once the onion and garlic are cooked, add the red peppers and cook for about another 5 minutes. Then add the homemade tomato sauce and let it cook over a low heat for 10 minutes. Finally, grind the mixture in a blender until it becomes a smooth, creamy sauce. Add a pinch of salt and sugar and serve with the roasted potatoes and sofrito.

7. Serve one or two slices of potato hot as a tapa in a small bowl.

PATATAS BRAVAS

Roasted Potatoes in a Paprika Sauce

This is another very popular tapa found everywhere in Spain. Spanish dishes are not normally very spicy. Patatas bravas are an exception and the sauce is often quite hot. There are several variations in cooking the potatoes. Sometimes they are par-boiled before roasting or frying in olive oil. The main thing to ensure is that the potatoes don't break up and remain in one piece, in cubes.

Ingredients:

> 3 tablespoons of olive oil
> 1 small onion, chopped
> 2 garlic cloves, chopped
> 225 g of chopped tomatoes
> 1 tablespoon of tomato purée
> 2 teaspoons of sweet paprika (pimentón dulce)
> A pinch of chilli powder and a pinch of sugar
> Chopped fresh parsley, to garnish

For the potatoes:

> 900 g of potatoes
> 2 tablespoons of olive oil

Preparation:

1. Fry the chopped onion in some olive oil for about 5 minutes until softened. Add the garlic, tomatoes, tomato purée, paprika, chilli powder, sugar and salt and bring to the boil, stirring. Simmer for about 10 minutes. Set aside for up to 24 hours.

2. Preheat the oven to 180°C.

3. Clean and cut the potatoes into small cubes of about 2 cm and dry them with kitchen paper. Spread the cubes on a roasting tin and add the olive oil.

4. Roast the potatoes for 40-50 minutes, until they are crisp and golden.

5. Put the potatoes into small dishes and spoon the reheated sauce over them. Sprinkle with parsley and serve.

PATATAS A LO POBRE

Fried Potatoes

This is an old, low-cost and simple dish, popular throughout rural Spain. It was often a nutritious and tasty alternative during periods of poverty. These days the dish is often served as a tapa or to accompany fried eggs or other dishes, instead of the traditional chips.

Because of its ingredients, it is obviously much more nutritious and tasty than ordinary French fried potatoes. There are lots of local variations of the dish in Spain and it is sometimes called "sartená de papas" or "papas al pelotón".

It is often served with either hard boiled or fried eggs.

Ingredients:

> 4-6 medium-sized potatoes
> 2 onions
> 1 red pepper
> 1 green pepper
> 4 cloves of garlic
> 1 tablespoon of olive oil
> 1 bay leaf
> Salt (to taste)

Preparation:

1. Cut the potatoes into slices with a thickness of about 0.5 cm.

2. Cut the onion and peppers into strips.

3. In a frying pan, stir-fry the onion with the garlic and peppers for about 4 minutes.

4. Add the potatoes to the frying pan along with the bay leaf and some salt to taste.

5. Cover and leave the pan on a medium heat for about 15 minutes, stirring the potatoes carefully without breaking them, to avoid sticking.

6. When they are tender, serve them hot.

PATATAS A LO POBRE CON NATA

Fried Potatoes with Cream

There are many variations on the popular dish "Patatas a lo Pobre". Here is one popular tapa variant, prepared with cream.

Ingredients:

4 potatoes
2 onions
300 ml of cream
2 peppers
Olive oil
Salt
Pepper

Preparation:

1. Peel and cut the potatoes into thin slices. Slice the onions.

2. Fry the potatoes and onions for about 15 minutes.

3. Cut the peppers into strips and add them to the potatoes and onions.

4. Add the cream and stir well to make sure everything is coated with cream.

5. Season with a little salt and pepper and leave to simmer for another fifteen minutes.

6. Serve hot in small bowls.

PATATAS A LO POBRE CON PIMIENTOS

Fried Potatoes with Peppers

Ingredients:

> 500 g of potatoes
> 2 onions
> 1 green pepper
> 1 red pepper
> Olive oil

Preparation:

1. Chop the onions and fry them in moderately hot olive oil.

2. Peel and wash the potatoes and slice them thinly.

3. When the onions starts to brown and become transparent, add the slices of potato with a little salt. Stir and turn to avoid sticking for about 15 minutes.

4. Cut the peppers into strips lengthwise (they can also be diced if you prefer). Add them to the pan as soon as the potatoes are browning.

5. Leave to simmer for 20 minutes, stirring occasionally.

6. Finely chop the parsley.

7. When all ingredients are well browned, add the parsley and add salt and pepper to your taste. Note: You can also crush a few cloves of garlic and add these to the mix or add a tablespoon of vinegar if you wish.

8. Serve hot on small plates.

PATATAS A LO POBRE CON TOMATE

Fried Potatoes with Tomato

Ingredients:

> 4 medium-sized potatoes
> 1 tomato
> 2 green peppers
> 1 onion
> Olive oil

Preparation:

1. Thinly slice the onion and fry in moderately hot olive oil.

2. Peel the potatoes and slice them.

3. When the onion starts to brown and become transparent, add the slices of potato with a little salt. Stir and turn to avoid sticking for about 15 minutes.

4. Dice the peppers and chop the tomatoes and add both to the pan when the potatoes are browning.

5. Stir well and leave to simmer for an additional 15 minutes.

6. Serve on small plates and garnish with fresh, finely chopped parsley.

PATATA CON QUESO DE OVEJA SEMICURADO
Baked Potato with Sheep Cheese

Ingredients:

> 2 large potatoes
> 1 clove of garlic, finely chopped
> Salt
> Dried parsley
> Dried thyme
> Olive oil
> 100 g of semi-mature sheep cheese
> Chopped fresh parsley

Preparation:

1. Peel the potatoes and cut them in half. Boil them in salted water for 2 minutes. Drain and place them on a baking tray lined with baking paper.

2. Season the potatoes with parsley, garlic and thyme. Coat them with olive oil and bake them for 25 min. in an oven preheated to 180°C.

3. Cut the cheese into thin slices and place these on each half of potato.

4. Put the potatoes back into the hot oven until the cheese melts.

5. Serve with a garnish of chopped fresh parsley.

PATATAS RELLENAS GRATINADAS

Gratinated Stuffed Potatoes

Ingredients:

Potatoes
Onion
Puréed tomatoes
Mushrooms
Courgette
Pepper
Olive oil
Salt
Béchamel sauce and/or grated cheese

Preparation:

1. Cut the potatoes in half and scoop out the potato to within a centimetre of the skin.

2. Place the potato halves on foil or baking paper to avoid sticking and bake them until they are soft.

3. While the potatoes are baking, make the filling and béchamel: For the filling, finely dice the potato that was scooped from the halves. Clean and dice the courgette, mushrooms and onion.

4. Fry the diced potato in one pan and the courgette, mushrooms and onion in another. When all the vegetables are cooked, mix them together in the same pan and add the puréed tomatoes. Continue to fry until cooked. Add a pinch of pepper and salt to taste.

5. When the potato "boats" are baked, fill each one with the vegetable mixture, and pour over the béchamel sauce (an alternative to béchamel is to use grated cheese and allow this to melt). Return the potatoes to the oven and allow them to gratinate until slightly brown. Serve hot on individual plates.

PATATAS REVOLCONAS

Potato and Paprika

Traditionally this tapa comes from Avila, Salamanca and Extremadura. This recipe is very simple, easy to prepare and is basically mashed potato, onion and paprika.

Ingredients:

> 1 kg of potatoes
> 1 red onion
> 2 bay leaves
> 3 cloves of garlic
> Half teaspoon of paprika
> Half teaspoon of cayenne pepper
> Olive oil
> A pinch of salt

Preparation:

1. Peel and chop the potatoes and boil them with a pinch of salt, the bay leaves, a whole onion and two tablespoons of olive oil. Once they are cooked, drain them and mash with a fork into a coarse purée.

2. Meanwhile, fry the garlic until golden in a little olive oil. Set aside.

3. Remove the pan from the heat and stir the paprika and the cayenne pepper into the oil. Put the pan on a low heat, add the mashed potatoes and thoroughly mix everything together.

4. Serve the potatoes in small individual portions with pieces of fresh bread or toast croutons.

---oOo---

2.7 Croquette Tapas

The definition of a croquette is a fried roll or ball of various ingredients coated in breadcrumbs. Many countries have their own variety of croquette, sometimes with different names.

The origin of the croquette is quite ancient. The Sicilian version ("arancini") dates from at least the 10th century CE. The popularity of this type of dish around the world (and especially in hot countries) certainly stems from the fact that waste food could be safely re-used as a croquette filling, because the high temperature of frying would kill any bacteria.

Whilst in most countries croquettes are often based on potato, this is not generally the case in Spain and in the Levantine countries. Spain has many varieties of croquette that are based on a vegetable filling mixed with a cheese or béchamel sauce.

The origins of Spain's croquettes can be found throughout the Middle East and Mediterranean to this day in the ever popular falafel and kubbeh, (a variant of which is the Sicilian "arancini" - fried rice balls). They are served in Aleppo in Syria with yoghurt (known as "kibbeh") and in Iraq with spicy tomato sauce known as "kubbat". These fried croquette-type dishes also spread to South America and the Caribbean with Levantine immigrants and are known as "quibe".

In the Middle East, these dishes are often served as part of a "mezze", which is a collection of small appetizer dishes; very much like a selection of tapas. In a similar way, croquettes in Spain are a very popular tapa dish and they come in all shapes, sizes and flavours. They are served alone, with a small salad, with bread or sometimes with a sauce.

There are many croquette recipes. Here we present some of the more popular, traditional vegetarian ones.

ALBÓNDIGAS DE ARROZ Y ESPINACAS
Rice and Spinach Balls

Both rice and spinach were introduced into Spain by the Arabs. Spinach was first cultivated in Persia and came to Spain in the 11th century CE. By the 15th century its cultivation and culinary use had spread throughout Europe.

In this recipe we make albóndigas (savoury balls) with rice and spinach with cheese. It can also be made without cheese.

The word albóndigas comes from the Arabic "al-bunduqa", meaning "ball". The Arabs brought this method of preparing food "balls" to Europe and they were later documented by the historian Luis del Mármol of Granada in 1573.

Ingredients

 1 kg of fresh spinach leaves
 140 ml of brown rice
 1 onion
 250 g of cheese (Manchego, for example)
 2 cloves of garlic
 2 tablespoons of red wine
 Flour and beaten egg (for coating)
 550 ml of tomato sauce (home-made)
 280 ml of cream
 280 ml of vegetable stock
 Olive oil for frying
 Breadcrumbs
 Salt
 Fresh parsley (for garnish)

Preparation:

1. Chop the garlic and onion and sauté them in a pan with a little olive oil.

2. Season and cook for 20 minutes.

3. In a separate saucepan boil the rice until tender.

4. Sauté the spinach in a saucepan with some olive oil for 4-5 minutes. Drain, chop the leaves and put aside.

5. Chop up the cheese and put it into a mixing bowl.

6. Add the cooked onion, garlic and chopped spinach and stir in with the cheese and the red wine.

7. Add the cooked rice and mix well together.

8. Shape the mixture into balls and coat each one with a mixture of beaten egg and flour and some breadcrumbs.

9. Deep fry the balls in a pan with plenty of olive oil. Drain and put aside to dry on some kitchen paper.

Sauce:

1. Mix the vegetable stock, the (home-made) tomato sauce and some cream in a saucepan.

2. Slowly heat for 8-10 minutes.

3. Add the rice/spinach balls to let them warm up again

4. Serve on a small dish and garnish with chopped fresh parsley.

CROQUETAS DE BERENJENA Y QUESO
Aubergine and Manchego Cheese Croquettes

Ingredients:

> 1 aubergine
> 80 g of butter
> Olive oil
> 100 g of cheese - Manchego or other strong cheese
> 100 g of wheat flour
> 250 ml of milk (at room temperature)
> 100 ml of cream
> White pepper
> 100 g of breadcrumbs
> 3 eggs, beaten
> Salt

Preparation:

1. Gently warm some olive oil in a frying pan and let the butter melt in it without letting it brown. Stir in the flour and continue to stir whilst gradually adding the milk. Season the mix with salt and pepper.

2. Let it simmer for 30 minutes, stirring regularly to prevent the mixture from burning then add the cheese and cream and cook for a further five minutes, continuously stirring.

3. Chop the aubergine and boil it in salted water until tender. Drain and add the pieces to the dough mixture. Put the mixture in a bowl to cool.

4. To make the croquettes, take a portion, roll it in flour, then in beaten egg and then in breadcrumbs.

5. Finally, fry in plenty of olive oil.

6. Serve alone or with a little salad.

CROQUETAS DE CABRALES

Croquettes of Cabrales Cheese of Asturias

Cabrales is a cheese made in a small area of Asturias, in the mountains of the Picos de Europa in the north of Spain. It is the result of an old artisan tradition by rural dairy farmers. The cheese can be made from pure, un-pasteurised cows' milk or blended in the traditional manner with goats' and/or sheep milk, which gives the cheese a stronger, spicier flavour. It is a matured, strong blue cheese and is protected under a European Designation of Origin (PDO).

Ingredients:

175 g of Cabrales cheese
3 tablespoons of flour
700 ml of milk
2 tablespoons of butter
1 egg
3 slices of bread
Olive oil, for frying
1 tablespoon of chopped parsley

Preparation:

1. Blend the cheese, flour and milk into a smooth paste.

2. Melt the butter in a frying pan. Add the prepared paste and cook it over a low heat, stirring constantly, for 15 minutes.

3. Put the mix into a bowl and allow it to cool.

4. Beat the egg in one bowl and crumble up the bread finely in another.

5. Take small portions of the chilled dough and mould these into rounded croquettes, dip them in the egg and roll them in the breadcrumbs.

6. Fry the croquettes in a pan with hot olive oil until golden brown.

7. Leave the croquettes to drain and then serve them sprinkled with finely-chopped fresh parsley.

CROQUETAS DE ESPINACAS Y PERA

Pear and Spinach Croquettes

Ingredients:

> 400 g of spinach (fresh or frozen)
> 300 ml of thick béchamel sauce
> 2 or 3 pears
> Pine kernels
> Breadcrumbs
> Chickpea flour
> Olive oil
> Black pepper
> Salt

Preparation:

1. Clean the spinach if it's fresh. Cook it in salted water until tender. Drain well and put aside.

2. Peel the pears and cook them for a few minutes.

3. Sauté a handful of pine kernels in a frying pan with a few drops of olive oil. Crush the pears with a fork and add them with the spinach to the kernels in the frying pan. Fry all together for a few minutes. Add salt and some ground black pepper to your taste.

4. Meanwhile, prepare a thick béchamel sauce. Remove from the heat and add the spinach mixture to the béchamel and mix well.

5. Let the mixture cool in the refrigerator for a few hours.

6. Make up a mixture of chickpea flour and water with the consistency of beaten egg.

7. To make the croquettes, take a tablespoonful of the mixture, dip it in the chickpea flour mix and then roll it in breadcrumbs. Mould the croquette into the shape you prefer and set aside to dry for a couple of minutes (this helps to keep them in one piece during frying).

8. Prepare a frying pan with hot olive oil. Fry the croquettes a few at a time. When golden brown, remove the croquettes and put them on a paper kitchen towel to soak up the excess oil.

9. Serve one or two croquettes per tapa, accompanied with a little salad and perhaps a piece of fresh bread.

CROQUETAS DE GARBANZOS - FALAFEL
Chickpea Croquettes

Chickpeas have been cultivated and eaten in Spain and the Middle East since the time of the Phoenicians and have long been a major source of protein. They remain a popular ingredient in hundreds of traditional dishes in Spain, including many tapas. This recipe for a chickpea croquette is similar to the traditional falafel recipe. Falafel is an extremely popular dish throughout the Middle East and has been served as a traditional street "fast food" for centuries, from Damascus to Marrakesh. It can be served by itself or with a variety of sauces, such as yoghurt with cucumber.

Ingredients:

> 400 g pre-cooked chickpeas, rinsed and drained
> 5 garlic cloves, chopped
> A handful of parsley
> 1 teaspoon of ground cumin
> 1 teaspoon of ground coriander
> Half a teaspoon of chilli powder
> 2 tablespoons of plain flour
> Olive oil for frying
> 1 small red onion, roughly chopped

Preparation:

1. Rinse and dry the chickpeas with kitchen paper.

2. Put the chickpeas in a blender along with the onion, garlic, parsley, spices, flour and a little salt. Blend until fairly smooth, and then shape the dough into round, cylindrical or spherical patties with your hands.

3. Heat the olive oil in a frying pan, add the falafels, and then quickly fry for 3 min. on all sides until lightly golden.

4. Serve with a little bread, a small salad and your choice of sauces. (Yoghurt sauces made with cucumber are very popular, as is home-made tomato sauce.)

CROQUETAS DE LENTEJAS Y PUERRO

Lentils and Leek Croquettes

A very similar recipe exists which substitutes leek for onion and yet another version uses chickpeas instead of lentils.

Ingredients:

> 400 g of cooked lentils (whole Castilian lentils)
> 1 leek
> 1 carrot
> 15 hazelnuts
> 1 teaspoon of olive oil
> 1 tablespoon of oregano
> Breadcrumbs
> Olive oil (in a spray)
> Salt

Preparation:

1. Finely chop the leek, the carrot and hazelnuts and fry all together in a frying pan with a teaspoon of olive oil.

2. Meanwhile, crush the lentils with a fork and add them to the mix in the pan. Season with oregano and salt. Stir well, remove from the heat and allow the mixture to cool.

3. When the mixture is lukewarm, make croquettes or patties by hand and coat them with breadcrumbs.

4. Cover a baking tray with baking paper, put the croquettes on it and spray with olive oil. Put them in an oven preheated to 190°C until golden brown (about 15 minutes).

5. Serve alone or with a slice of bread or with a little salad and alioli sauce.

CROQUETAS DE PATATA, ESPINACAS Y QUESO

Croquettes with Potato, Spinach and Cheese

Ingredients:

> 4 large potatoes
> 150 g of fresh spinach
> 200 g of grated cheese
> 2 eggs (beaten)
> Breadcrumbs
> Olive oil
> Salt and pepper to taste

Preparation:

1. Cook the potatoes in their skins in salted water, leave them to cool, peel them, mash them and pass them through a purée mill. Put aside.

2. Clean the spinach and boil it in salted water for a few minutes. Drain it, let it cool, and chop it up.

3. Mix the potatoes and spinach, add the grated cheese and mix all into a dough. Season it with salt and pepper.

4. Oil your hands. Take small portions of the dough and form balls of about 3 cm in diameter. Dip these in beaten egg and roll in breadcrumbs and then repeat the coating in egg and breadcrumbs.

5. Fry the croquettes in plenty of olive oil.

6. When they are golden brown place them on kitchen paper to drain.

7. Serve them hot on individual plates with a little green salad.

CROQUETAS DE PUERRO

Leek Croquettes

Ingredients:

> 250 g of leeks
> 25 ml of vegetable stock
> 10 g of butter
> 10 g of flour
> 100 ml of milk
> 100 g of breadcrumbs
> 100 ml of olive oil for frying
> 3 eggs, beaten
> 1 tablespoon of chopped fresh parsley

Preparation:

1. Cut the leek roughly and fry in olive oil for 6-8 minutes. Add the vegetable broth and leave to simmer for 15 minutes.

2. Make a thick béchamel sauce by slowly melting the butter in a pan, stir in the flour until browned and then slowly add the milk and a pinch of salt.

3. Mix the leeks with the béchamel sauce and allow the mixture to cool.

4. Make small croquettes by hand, coat them in egg and roll them in breadcrumbs.

5. Fry them carefully in plenty of olive oil, trying to ensure they do not break up. Drain on paper towels.

6. Serve hot, sprinkled with fresh parsley.

CROQUETAS DE SETAS

Mushroom Croquettes

Ingredients:

> 200 g of mixed mushrooms
> Half an onion
> 4 tablespoons of flour
> 4 tablespoons of butter
> 500 ml of milk
> Salt, pepper, nutmeg, parsley, garlic powder, to your taste
> Olive oil
> Egg (beaten)
> Breadcrumbs

Preparation:

1. Sauté the very finely chopped onion in a pan with the butter. Chop the mushrooms quite small and add them to the onion.

2. Season with salt and pepper, nutmeg and parsley and add some garlic powder.

3. Stir in the flour and let it brown a little. Slowly incorporate the milk, stirring continuously, until it has the right consistency (the mixture should not stick to the sides of the pan).

4. Season the mix with salt, remove from the heat and let it cool down in a bowl.

5. Make the croquettes by hand as you prefer (round, spherical or cylindrical). Dip them in beaten egg and roll them in breadcrumbs.

6. Fry in plenty of hot olive oil.

7. Let the croquettes drain on paper towels.

8. Serve hot, garnished with fresh parsley, with a light mayonnaise or alioli.

CROQUETAS DE ZANAHORIA
Carrot Croquettes

Ingredients:

> 500 g of carrots
> Half an onion
> 100 g of flour
> 1 litre of milk
> 2 eggs (beaten)
> Breadcrumbs
> Olive oil
> Salt
> Mustard
> Black pepper

Preparation:

1. Peel the carrots and chop them into very small pieces. Finely cut up the onion.

2. Gently fry the carrots and onions in a pan with a little olive oil and let them cook for 10 minutes over a medium heat. After that, stir in the flour and mix everything well, leaving the mixture to thoroughly cook for another 2 or 3 minutes, stirring constantly.

3. Heat the milk in a saucepan. When it is heated, gradually add it to the mixture in the frying pan, stirring constantly until obtaining a creamy paste. Add salt to taste. Stir the mixture until it does not stick to the pan.

4. Remove the paste from the heat and place it in a bowl with a lid. After 10 minutes of cooling, seal the container and put it in the fridge. Ideally, leave the mix for one day, but as a minimum, leave it for 3 hours in the refrigerator.

5. Mould the croquettes in a roll shape and coat them in beaten egg and breadcrumbs.

6. Fry the croquettes in a pan with plenty of olive oil. When they are golden brown, take them out of the pan and briefly leave them to drain on kitchen paper to remove excess oil. Serve with a little salad and a mustard sauce.

---oOo---

2.8 Rice and Pasta Tapas

ALUBIAS CON ARROZ

Beans with Rice

Ingredients:

0.5 kg of beans (pinto, white or red beans)
2 large cloves of garlic
1 bay (laurel) leaf
2-3 tablespoons of olive oil
1 onion
1 red pepper
1 tablespoon of unbleached white flour
1 tablespoon of sweet (Spanish) paprika
Salt
500 ml of cooked long-grain white rice

Preparation:

1. Place the beans in a large saucepan and cover them with water. Leave them to soak overnight.

2. Drain the water from the beans the following day, and pour enough fresh water into the saucepan to ensure there is about 2 cm of water above the beans. Bring to the boil. Add the bay leaf. Reduce the heat and leave to simmer.

3. Chop the onion and the red pepper. Cut the garlic cloves into quarters. Pour 2-3 tablespoons of olive oil into a frying pan and put it on a medium heat. When the oil is hot, add the onion, pepper and garlic and brown for about 5 minutes.

4. Once the onion is browned, stir in the flour. Add 2-3 tablespoons of broth from the bean pot to the frying pan and mix the ingredients. Add a tablespoon of paprika to this "sauce" and mix thoroughly. Add it to the pot of beans and stir.

5. While the beans are simmering, prepare the white rice.

6. Continue to cook until the beans are soft, but not mushy. Add salt to taste. Check the pot regularly. You may need to add water to the beans.

Some prefer to serve the beans with their broth - more like soup -, while others prefer to serve it as a thicker bean dish.

7. Add the boiled rice and serve in small bowls.

ARROZ CALDOSO

Rice and Bean Stew

This is a very typical Spanish dish, often served as a winter tapa. In particular the use of the ñora (a famous dried, round, red pepper) is typical of the cuisine of the areas of Murcia and Alicante in the South East of the country where this recipe originates. The peppers are dried in the sun and used as a condiment in many fried dishes. It has a characteristic sweet taste.

There is an endless set of variants for this recipe, including how much water we use in the broth to determine how thick or thin we want the dish to be. In this you have to suit your own tastes.

Ingredients:

> 50 g of lentils
> 50 g of chickpeas
> 50 g of pinto beans
> 50 g of white beans
> 1 "cardo" thistle (cardoon)
> 100 g of spinach
> 100 g of chard
> 1 turnip
> 1 carrot
> 1 ñora pepper
> 200 g of rice
> 12 almonds
> 1 slice of old bread
> 1 onion
> Olive oil
> 1 dried tomato

Preparation:

1. Let the pulses (lentils, chickpeas, pinto and white beans) soak for 12 hours.

2. Put the pulses in a saucepan, together with the dried tomato, the chopped turnip and carrot, sliced chard, sliced spinach leaf, and the cleaned thistle.

3. Fill the pan with water (depending on the consistency you prefer, you can make it more or less water). Add salt to taste.

4. In the meantime, fry the almonds, ñora pepper and the slice of bread in a frying pan. When ready, put the mixture in a mortar, grind it together and put aside.

5. In the same oil, fry the onion until golden brown and then put it directly into the saucepan with the vegetables.

6. After boiling for two hours add the contents of the mortar and boil for another hour.

7. Finally add the rice, let it boil for 15 minutes and then turn off the heat.

8. Serve hot in small bowls with a slice of fresh bread.

ARROZ VEGETARIANO AL HORNO

Baked Rice with Vegetables

Ingredients:

> 300 g of rice
> 1 courgette
> 1 small aubergine
> 1 leek
> 1 carrot
> 1 green pepper
> 1 red pepper
> Vegetable stock

Preparation:

1. Preheat the oven to 200°C.

2. Finely chop all the vegetables and fry them in a flameproof casserole for a few minutes.

3. When they are fried, add the rice and sauté.

4. Add the vegetable stock: Two parts stock to one part rice.

5. Put the dish in the oven for about 20 minutes. Serve hot in small portions (using a small mould), decorated with strips of raw carrot.

ENSALADA DE PASTA CON BERENJENAS, TOMATES, ACEITUNAS Y QUESO

Pasta Salad with Aubergine, Tomatoes, Olives and Goats' Cheese

---

Ingredients:

> 1100 ml of whole wheat pasta spirals, cooked, drained and cooled
> 70 ml of olive oil
> 400 ml of aubergine, cut into thick sticks
> 4 cloves of garlic, thinly sliced
> Coarse sea salt
> 200 ml of dried tomatoes in olive oil
> 200 ml of black olives without stones
> 280 ml of diced fresh goats' cheese, marinated in olive oil with herbs
> Dried oregano
> Dried red pepper in flakes

Preparation:

1. Sauté the garlic in the olive oil for 2-3 minutes on a medium heat, until it begins to brown.

2. Add the aubergine and sauté, stirring occasionally, until it begins to brown, about 6-8 minutes. Add salt to taste.

3. Place the cooked pasta in a bowl and add the aubergine, pieces of dried tomato, the olives and stir.

4. Sprinkle with a little oregano and flakes of dried red pepper to taste.

5. Serve in small portions with little blocks of marinated fresh goats' cheese (or any other feta type cheese).

ENSALADA DE PASTA CON SALMOREJO

Pasta Salad with Salmorejo Sauce

Ingredients:

> 400 g of pasta suitable for a salad
> Salmorejo sauce (see the recipe under sauces)
> Sliced aubergine
> Olive oil to fry
> Manchego cheese in very fine flakes
> Fresh basil

Preparation:

1. Cook the pasta until tender, drain and put it in a salad bowl.

2. Prepare some salmorejo sauce (see recipe under sauces). Add to the pasta and mix together well.

3. Fry some slices of aubergine in olive oil. When browned, drain them and add them to the salad.

4. Slice some Manchego cheese very finely. Serve the pasta in small bowls, decorated with some basil and a few thin slices of cheese.

FIDEOS A LO POBRE CON PIMIENTOS Y HIERBAS

Noodles with Peppers and Herbs

Here is a simple traditional recipe from the Islas Canarias, sometimes served as a tapa.

Ingredients:

> 400 g of noodles
> 100 g of breadcrumbs
> Red peppers
> 2 cloves of garlic
> Cayenne pepper (to taste)
> Salt
> Parsley
> Oregano

Preparation:

1. Boil the pasta in a saucepan with water and salt for about 10 minutes ("al dente"). Drain and put aside.

2. Finely chop and fry the garlic in a little olive oil. When the garlic begins to turn brown, add the breadcrumbs and fry until golden brown.

3. Simultaneously, wrap the peppers in foil and roast them in the oven. When they are roasted, peel them and cut them into strips. Add these to the pan with the garlic and breadcrumbs. Fry the mixture together for 5 minutes.

4. Take the cooked pasta and stir it into the bread crumb mix. Sprinkle with some oregano and cayenne, and cook for a further 3 minutes.

5. Serve hot in a small dish with a little chopped fresh parsley.

PAELLA DE COLIFLOR, HABAS, CHAMPIÑONES Y CÚRCUMA

Paella of Cauliflower, Broad beans, Mushrooms and Turmeric

Ingredients:

> 300 g of round brown rice
> 1 small cauliflower
> 500 g of broad beans
> 200 g of mushrooms
> 1 small onion
> 1 red pepper
> 4 cloves of garlic
> 2 tomatoes
> 50 ml of olive oil
> 1 teaspoon of turmeric
> Salt
> Vegetable stock

Preparation:

1. Clean and cut the vegetables: dice the pepper and the onion, slice the mushrooms, divide the cauliflower into small florets, shell the broad beans, and crush the garlic.

2. Make the sofrito by frying the pepper, onion, garlic and tomato in the olive oil in a paella pan or a large frying pan.

3. Stir the cauliflower, the mushrooms and the broad beans into the sofrito, then add the rice, heat for a couple of minutes and then add some hot vegetable stock (or water), using three parts of liquid to one part of rice.

4. Add the turmeric and salt and cook over a medium heat for about 20 minutes, or until the rice is tender (depending on the rice). If necessary, add more stock whilst cooking.

5. Once the rice is cooked, cover the pan and let the paella stand for about 5 minutes. Serve warm in small bowls with a wedge of lemon.

PAELLA DE VERDURAS

Vegetable Paella

Whilst paella is often made in large quantities for communal or family parties, it is also an easy-to-make and very popular tapa dish.

Ingredients:

> 100 g of leeks
> 100 g of onion
> 150 g of mushrooms
> 150 g of cabbage
> 150 g of peas (frozen)
> 150 g of green beans
> 150 g of baby carrots (frozen)
> 100 g of broccoli
> 1 red pepper
> 1 vegetable stock cube in 1 litre of water
> 3 strands of saffron
> 2 tablespoons of homemade tomato sauce
> 475 g of round rice
> 1 squeeze of lemon
> 150 ml of olive oil
> Salt - a pinch
> Black olives (without stones)
> 1 hard-boiled egg

Preparation:

1. Clean all the vegetables. Then chop the leaks in slices (white part only). Finely chop the onion. Slice the mushrooms thinly. Cut the cabbage into strips. Pre-cook the baby carrots and peas (or use frozen). Dice the green beans. Slice the red pepper into strips. Divide the broccoli into florets.

2. Pre-heat the oven to 180°C.

3. Make a simple tomato sauce by puréeing some tomatoes.

4. Pour 50 ml of olive oil into a large frying pan or use a special paella pan (called a "paellera") and sauté the leeks, onion and mushrooms until all the liquid has evaporated.

5. Cook the remaining vegetables in another saucepan until they are almost tender and then add them to the sautéed leeks, onions and mushrooms in the paellera.

6. Then put the rice and the remaining olive oil into the paellera and fry until the rice becomes opaque.

7. Add the lemon juice and season generously.

8. Add hot vegetable stock (or just water) and when it boils put the pan into the oven at 180 degrees for 20 minutes. Check whether the rice is cooked. If it's still hard, cover and continue to cook for a further 5 minutes.

9. Serve the paella tapas in small bowls, garnished with strips of red pepper, half olives and a slice of boiled egg.

---oOo---

2.9 Tapas made with Beans, Nuts, Lentils and Chickpeas

ALMENDRAS SALADAS

Salted Almonds

Ingredients:

> 260 ml of blanched almonds
> 1 teaspoon of sea salt
> 1/2 teaspoon of sweet paprika powder
> Olive oil, for frying

Preparation:

1. Pour about 2cm of olive oil into a saucepan and heat to about 190°C

2. Fry the almonds until lightly golden.

3. Drain, sprinkle with the salt and paprika and mix well.

4. Place in small bowl as a tapa.

ALUBIAS NEGRAS CON ARROZ - "MOROS Y CRISTIANOS"

Black Beans and Rice

Black beans and rice is a popular dish, eaten in las Islas Canarias. The name recalls the great struggles between the Muslim Moors and the Christians in Spanish history. The tender black beans symbolize the Moors, and the white rice the Christians.

Ingredients:

> 15 ml of olive oil
> 1 small onion, finely chopped
> 1 medium-sized green pepper, finely chopped
> 4 cloves of garlic, finely chopped
> Half a teaspoon of dried oregano
> 450 ml of cooked black beans
> Preserve the cooking broth from the black beans
> 1 bay leaf
> 220 ml of long grain rice
> 1 teaspoon of white distilled vinegar

Preparation:

1. Heat some olive oil in a medium-sized pan over a medium heat. Add the onions and peppers and cook them for about 10 minutes until soft. Stir in the crushed garlic and oregano, and leave to cook for about 1 minute more.

2. Use the cooking broth from the black beans. Add enough water to bring the volume up to about 500 ml. Add the liquid and bay leaf to the vegetable pot and when it boils, stir in the black beans and rice. Bring it back to the boil.

3. Reduce the heat to medium-low. Simmer, covered, until the rice absorbs all the water, about 25 minutes. Add vinegar and stir.

4. Remove the pan from the heat and leave it to stand for about 5 minutes more.

5. Divide the rice and beans in small serving bowls and add a few drops of olive oil. Garnish with fresh parsley.

ALUBIAS CON QUESO

Beans with Goats' Cheese

This is a healthy, tasty dish which is sometimes served as a starter, but also makes a delicious tapa. You can use large butter beans or the smaller white bean. The cheese you select depends on your own taste. Traditionally, the dish is served with fresh or young goats' cheese, but you can also use a more mature goats' or sheep cheese.

Ingredients:

> 350 g of white beans, pre-cooked and drained
> 90 g of fresh goats' cheese
> 2 carrots
> 1 red pepper
> Half a small onion
> 2 bay leaves
> Sweet smoked paprika powder
> Water
> Salt
> Olive oil

Preparation:

1. Peel and coarsely chop the carrots, dice the pepper and cut the onion into 6 pieces. Cook these ingredients in a saucepan with just enough water to cover, together with the bay leaves and salt to taste.

2. After about 10 minutes cooking, blend the onion, carrots, a small part of the pepper and a little scoop of the cooking liquid together, until you have a creamy sauce. Then put this back in the saucepan.

3. Drain the pre-cooked beans and add them to the sauce in the pan. Stir in half a teaspoon of smoked paprika powder, and leave all to simmer for about 5 minutes so that the beans take up the flavour of the sauce.

5. Remove the bay leaves and serve the beans in small bowls with a generous scattering of fresh goat cheese. Add a drop of olive oil, and garnish with a dusting of paprika powder.

It can be served as a hot tapa in winter and at room temperature in the summer.

CAZUELA DE GARBANZOS

Chickpea Casserole

This is a perfect tapas recipe for the cold months of winter.

Ingredients:

> 300 g of chickpeas
> 250 g of French beans
> 3 carrots
> 200 g of pumpkin
> 2 potatoes
> 2 ripe tomatoes
> 1 green pepper
> 1 onion
> 200 g of almonds (blanched)
> 1 tablespoon of vinegar
> 1 slice of bread
> 1 head of garlic
> Saffron
> 1 bay leaf

Preparation:

1. Leave the chickpeas to soak overnight. The next day, drain them and put them in a saucepan with the skinned and halved tomatoes, onion, the green pepper and the carrots - all finely diced.

2. Clean the garlic head and add it to the pot. Clean the green beans and remove the hard stem. Chop them and add them to the other vegetables, together with a bay leaf and a drop of olive oil. Add water to cover the ingredients and put the saucepan on the heat.

3. While these vegetables are cooking, peel and dice the pumpkin and the potatoes. Put them aside.

4. Put a slice of bread soaked in vinegar into a mortar along with the almonds and some saffron. Grind them well together.

5. When the chickpeas begin to soften, add the pumpkin and 5 minutes later the potatoes and the mix from the mortar. Season to your taste and let it simmer for about 20 minutes. There should be a little broth left when it is ready.

6. Serve hot in small bowls with a little bread.

GARBANZOS CON ESPINACAS A LA CREMA
Chickpeas with Creamed Spinach

This recipe can be made very quickly using previously cooked chickpeas. This tapa is also delicious if you add some pine kernels or raisins, to create a different and interesting taste.

Ingredients:

>600 g of cooked and drained chickpeas
>300 g of fresh spinach
>2-3 large cloves of garlic
>400 ml of evaporated milk
>Nutmeg
>Black pepper
>Salt
>Olive oil
>Paprika powder

Preparation:

1. Peel and chop the garlic. Pour some olive oil into a large frying pan and sauté the garlic. When they start to turn golden brown, add the chickpeas and sauté for a few more minutes with a pinch of freshly ground black pepper and salt.

2. Mix in the fresh spinach bit by bit and when it has lost its volume, take out the chickpeas and spinach and leave aside.

3. Pour the evaporated milk into the same pan, bring it to the boil and then reduce the heat, stirring constantly. Cook until it begins to reduce. Add a little nutmeg, salt and freshly ground black pepper.

4. When the evaporated milk is creamy, return the chickpeas and spinach to the pan and cook everything together for a couple of minutes.

5. The creamed chickpeas and spinach are served in small bowls with a sprinkling of paprika powder.

GARBANZOS CON ESPINACAS Y TOMATE

Chickpeas with Spinach and Tomato

This is a delicious recipe from the Triana barrio of Sevilla and the dish can be found on many tapas menus in the city.

Ingredients:

A bunch of spinach
About 400 grams of cooked chickpeas
1 onion, chopped
1 green pepper
1 clove of garlic, finely chopped
3 tomatoes, finely chopped
Paprika powder
Olive oil
Pepper (to taste)
Cumin (to taste)
Salt

Preparation:

1. Wash the spinach leaves and cook them in a little salted water. Boil until just tender - no more.

2. Boil the (soaked) chickpeas in salted water. If you are using pre-cooked chickpeas, rinse them well under running water. Put them aside when cooked.

3. Fry the garlic, onion and pepper, all finely chopped and in this order in a frying pan with a little olive oil. As they start to brown, remove from the heat and mix in a tablespoon of paprika powder. Stir well to prevent burning.

4. Add the peeled and finely chopped tomatoes. Then mix in the spinach, chickpeas, pepper and cumin (to your taste), cover the pan and simmer it over a low heat until the broth is reduced and the flavours completely mingled.

5. Serve in small bowls with a slice of bread or toast.

GARBANZOS CON HINOJO Y NARANJA

Chickpeas with Grilled Fennel and Orange

This is a typical dish designed to use whatever is left over in the kitchen. Fennel is found growing wild throughout most of Spain and chickpeas are a staple of the Spanish diet. Add a couple of oranges, some imagination, olive oil and some chilli powder and you have a nutritious tapa with an interesting and tasty combination of flavours. If you don't have a fennel bulb you can pick some wild fennel to add flavour instead.

Ingredients:

> 300 g of cooked chickpeas
> 1 fennel bulb
> 2 oranges
> Freshly ground black pepper
> Chilli powder (to your taste)
> Olive oil
> Salt

Preparation:

1. Clean and peel the fennel bulb. Cut it into slices and put aside. Peel the oranges with a knife and cut them into slices. Drain the cooked (or pre-cooked) chickpeas.

2. Put a little olive oil on the grill and firstly grill the slices of fennel with a little salt to taste. When they are roasted slightly, turn them over and add the orange slices, sauté until golden on both sides.

3. Remove the fennel and orange slices from the grill and grill the chickpeas in the remaining juices. Add a little olive oil if necessary. Season with freshly ground black pepper and chilli powder and then sauté for a few minutes. Finally, mix all the ingredients together well and serve the sautéed chickpeas, grilled fennel and orange in a small bowl with a little drop of olive oil and some salad.

GARBANZOS CON QUESO DE CABRA Y PIMIENTOS

Chickpeas with Goats' Cheese and Peppers

This tapa of chickpeas with goats' cheese and peppers is nutritious and tasty. It is easy to make.

Ingredients:

> 400 g of cooked chickpeas
> 1 - 2 green peppers
> 1 - 2 red peppers
> 1 onion
> 5 cloves of garlic
> 200 g of goats' cheese
> A splash of milk (enough to make the melted cheese creamy)
> 1 teaspoon of harissa paste (a chilli paste from Morocco)
> 1 teaspoon of dried mint
> 1 teaspoon of oregano
> Allspice
> Olive oil
> Salt

Preparation:

1. The chickpeas should be prepared in advance, which may mean overnight soaking and then cooking, but you can also use a jar of cooked chickpeas.

2. Prepare the peppers by cutting them in half, removing the stalk and seeds. Cut them lengthwise into thin strips. Peel the onion and dice finely. Peel the cloves of garlic and cut them into thin slices.

3. Pour some olive oil into a frying pan, put it on the heat, add the peppers with some salt to taste and let them simmer. When the peppers begin to soften, add the onion, the oregano and a little allspice. When the onion is transparent, add three of the sliced cloves of garlic. Check to see if it needs more salt and continue the simmering until the peppers are cooked to your liking.

4. In a separate frying pan, brown the rest of the garlic in a little olive oil and then stir in the chickpeas and the harissa paste. When all is well mixed, incorporate the chopped goats' cheese to melt. Finally, add a splash of milk and the dried mint, and, if necessary, another pinch of salt.

5. Cook for about five minutes over a medium heat until all ingredients are well mixed and the chickpeas are covered with the creamed goats' cheese.

6. Serve the chickpeas in small dishes on a bed of the red and green peppers, decorated with a few leaves of fresh mint and, if you like, a few drops of mint-flavoured olive oil.

GARBANZOS TOSTADOS

Roasted Chickpeas

This is a traditional Barcelona "street snack" and tapa. It is much less hard to eat than the toasted chickpeas you buy in the shop!

Any type of chickpea can be used, large or small, provided they are of good quality and well cooked. There are a lot of variants of this tapa using all kinds of different herbs and spices such as Hierbes de Provence, chilli powder, curry, etc. The amount and type of herbs, spices and salt you add is up to you.

Ingredients:

>Cooked chickpeas
>Ginger, Cumin, Garlic powder, Oregano
>Olive oil
>Salt

Preparation:

1. Cook the chickpeas (or use pre-cooked chickpeas). Wash them, drain them well and spread them on a tray. Leave the chickpeas to dry at room temperature for a few hours.

2. Preheat the oven to 200°C.

3. Prepare the spice mix you are going to use and add salt to taste. Sprinkle the mixture over the chickpeas and add a little olive oil. Mix well.

4. When the oven is hot, put in the tray with the chickpeas (well spread). Bake for about 30 minutes, moving the chickpeas around a couple of times. The chickpeas should be slightly crunchy, not soft and not too hard, so check them regularly.

5. When they are almost ready, turn off the oven and let the chickpeas cool in the oven. If you want to serve them immediately, you can remove them from the oven and let them cool down at room temperature.

6. Serve the roasted chickpeas warm in a small bowl as a tapa. Any surplus chickpeas can be stored in a jar with a tight lid. They can be kept for several days

GUISO DE LENTEJAS

Lentil Stew

Lentil stew is a popular and traditional dish in Spain and makes a warming tapa in the cold winter months. You can also add any type of vegetable you have to hand - normally it is potato and carrot, but you can add any leftover vegetables you may have, like cauliflower, broccoli etc.

Ingredients:

> 1 large onion, chopped
> 4 cloves of garlic, finely chopped
> 1 kilo of chopped vegetables, including potatoes and carrots
> 420 g of diced tomatoes
> 420 g of cooked lentils
> 1 litre of vegetable broth
> 1.25 teaspoon of dried oregano
> 0.5 teaspoon of paprika powder
> 0.5 teaspoon of ground cumin
> 60 g of quinoa (optional)
> 160 g of cooked pumpkin
> Salt and Freshly ground black pepper

Preparation:

1. Fry the onion in a large frying pan until it begins to brown. Stir in the garlic and cook for about 1 minute.

2. Add the vegetable broth, vegetables, tomatoes, pre-cooked lentils, the oregano, paprika and cumin and cook until the broth begins to boil.

3. Mix in the quinoa and cook over a medium heat for about 15 minutes until it is tender.

4. Add the pumpkin, and season to taste.

5. Cook for a further 5 minutes (adding more water if necessary).

6. Serve hot, garnished with some parsley and rosemary leaves in small bowls with a little piece of bread.

LENTEJAS CON ARROZ Y CEBOLLAS CARAMELIZADAS

Lentils with Rice and Caramelized Onions

Ingredients:

>4 tablespoons of olive oil
>1 white onion, finely chopped
>2 white onions, cut into thin slices
>3 cloves of garlic
>2 teaspoons of ground cumin
>1 teaspoon of ground cinnamon
>900 ml of vegetable stock (see recipe to make your own)
>150 g of cooked lentils
>150 g of rice
>2 tablespoons of butter
>Pepper to taste

Preparation:

1. Fry the chopped onion with the garlic, cumin, cinnamon and pepper in a large frying pan in olive oil for about 4 minutes or until the onion is tender.

2. Add a little salt to taste.

3. Add the vegetable stock and the lentils and bring to the boil.

4. Reduce the heat to medium-low, cover the pan and simmer the lentils for about 10 minutes.

5. Add the rice and bring all back to the boil over a high heat.

6. Reduce the heat to medium-low and cover the pot. Cook the rice with the lentils for a further 15 minutes, until all the broth is absorbed.

7. Meanwhile, put a large frying pan on medium heat and melt the butter. Sauté the sliced onions for 20 minutes or until caramelized.

8. Stir the rice and lentils with a fork to separate the grains.

10. Serve the rice and lentils hot in small dishes, decorated with the caramelized onions.

LENTEJAS VIUDAS CON ARROZ

Widow's Lentil Stew with Rice

There are many such "widow's stews" in Spain. The "widow" refers to the fact that they do not contain meat. The reasons for the absence of meat may be religious, seasonal or economic - or a mixture of all three!

This is just one of those typical and healthy lentil dishes with rice and vegetables. It is a perfect vegetarian tapa for the cold winter months.

Ingredients:

> 200 g of small brown lentils ("Pardina"), well washed
> 75 g - 100 g of rice
> 2 carrots
> 1 onion
> 1 head of garlic
> 2 potatoes
> 2 to 3 bay leaves
> Salt
> Smoked paprika powder
> Olive oil
> Water
> 1 vegetable stock cube

Preparation:

1. Peel the vegetables. Chop the carrots into thick slices and dice the potatoes. Cut the onions in eighths. Leave the head of the garlic whole. It can be removed at the end of cooking, if you wish.

2. Sauté the onions in a frying pan with a little olive oil. When they are browned, add the carrots and potatoes to the pan. Turn the ingredients in the pan over a few times and when they begin to brown add the bay leaf, salt and pepper. Sauté well and then add about 2 litres of water with the vegetable stock cube (or 2 litres of homemade vegetable broth) and the lentils.

3. After about 15 minutes, stir in the rice. Let the rice cook through for about 15-20 minutes. Serve hot in small bowls with a little bread.

---oOo---

2.10 Salad Tapas

ENSALADA DE ALUBIAS CON PESTO

Bean and Pesto Salad

Salads based on chickpeas, various beans or lentils are a good way to continue enjoying pulses during the hottest months of summer when you don't feel like traditional stews. In this recipe we add some pesto - which is also found in Spain (generally in Cataluña, Valencia and the Baleares Islands).

Ingredients:

> 200 g of cooked white beans
> 200 g of tomatoes
> 1 celery stick
> 2 tablespoons of fresh parsley leaves
> 1 onion (or a spring onion)
> Half a red pepper
> 3 tablespoons of olive oil
> Salt
> Black pepper
> 1 tablespoon of white wine vinegar

For the pesto:

> 20-30 g of fresh basil leaves
> 200 g of olive oil
> Half a teaspoon of salt
> 2 garlic cloves
> 40 g of grated cheese (optional)
> Pinch of ground pepper

Preparation:

1. Prepare the pesto by blending the basil with the oil, the salt, the peeled garlic, the grated cheese and a little ground pepper in a food processor. Don't overblend it – it should keep a little texture. Keep the pesto in the fridge until ready to serve.

2. Mix the cooked and drained beans in a salad bowl together with the chopped tomato, finely chopped celery, chopped parsley, and the diced onion and pepper.

3. Dress the salad with olive oil, a little salt, pepper and vinegar, stirring to mix it all together well. Put it in the fridge until ready to serve.

4. Serve the salad in small bowls with a teaspoonful of pesto on each serving, accompanied by bread.

ENSALADA DE ALUBIAS CON SALSA VINAGRETA
White Bean Salad with Vinaigrette Sauce

White bean salad with vinaigrette sauce is a simple and quick tapa, especially good for the summertime. White beans are simply combined with onion, pepper, oil and vinegar. You can also use red kidney beans, of course.

Ingredients:

> 500 ml of cooked small white kidney beans
> Half a red pepper
> Half a green pepper
> 1 small onion
> 6 tablespoons of red wine vinegar
> 70 ml of olive oil
> Salt to taste
> 1 or 2 cloves of garlic (to your taste)

Preparation:

1. Drain and rinse the cooked beans.

2. Finely chop the peppers, garlic and onion and place them into a mixing bowl. Add the beans and mix.

3. Stir in the vinegar, the olive oil and salt. Taste and adjust flavour with salt.

4. Serve in a small bowl with some crispy bread.

ENSALADA DE CEBOLLETAS Y APIO DE MORATALLA

Celery and Spring Onion Salad of Moratalla

This is a traditional spring onion and celery salad from the town of Moratalla in Murcia.

Ingredients:

>3 large spring onions, finely sliced
>60 ml of lemon juice
>4 large tomatoes, roughly chopped
>1 bunch of celery, cut into 1 cm pieces
>A pinch of ground white pepper
>A pinch of ground cloves
>90 ml of olive oil
>1 tablespoon of cider vinegar
>Salt to taste

Preparation:

1. Leave the spring onions to marinate in lemon juice with salt for about an hour in the refrigerator.

2. Place all the remaining ingredients in a salad bowl. Toss the ingredients well until completely mixed. When the spring onions are marinated, stir them into the mix, together with the lemon juice.

3. Serve in small bowls with a slice of bread.

ENSALADA DE GARBANZOS, TOMATES Y QUESO DE CABRA

Chickpea, Tomato and Goats' Cheese Salad

Ingredients:

> 150 g of dried chickpeas
> 200 g of cherry tomatoes
> 200 g of fresh goats' cheese
> 1 red onion (or 1 small spring onion)
> 1 teaspoon of sugar
> 1 teaspoon of oregano
> 4 tablespoons of olive oil
> 1 bay leaf
> Parsley, fresh
> 1 lemon
> Salt
> Pepper

Preparation:

1. Leave the chickpeas to soak overnight. Rinse them and boil them in a saucepan with water and a bay leaf. Simmer over a low heat for about 1 hour. Remove the pan from the heat and let the chickpeas cool. You can also use pre-cooked chickpeas from a jar.

2. Cut the cheese into small cubes. Wash the tomatoes and cut them in half. Peel the onion and chop finely. Wash the lemon, dry it, grate the skin and squeeze the juice. Wash the parsley, leave it to dry and chop it very finely.

3. Vinaigrette: carefully heat the sugar with 2 tablespoons of water and the lemon zest. Remove from the heat and add 2 tablespoons of lemon juice, the oil, oregano, and 2 tablespoons of chopped parsley. Add salt and pepper.

4. Drain the chickpeas and mix with the tomato, cheese, onion and vinaigrette.

5. Serve cold in small dishes with a little bread.

ENSALADA DE LENTEJAS (TABULÉ)

Lentil Salad (Tabbouleh)

Tabbouleh is a salad made throughout the Levantine and Mediterranean. It is a traditional component of the "mezze", the Arabic equivalent of tapas. Versions of tabbouleh can be found from Baghdad, through Turkey, Cyprus, Armenia, Syria, Palestine, through to Morocco. The dish has its origins in the middle ages and can be made with bulgur, couscous or lentils and a wide variety of salad ingredients. This is a Spanish variant.

Ingredients:

> 80 g of dried, small lentils "pardinas"
> 100 g of tomato
> 50 g of onion
> Half a small cucumber
> Juice of half a lemon
> 10 mint leaves, finely chopped
> 1 teaspoon of parsley, finely chopped
> Coriander, to taste
> Salt

Preparation:

1. Soak the lentils for a few hours. Cook the lentils until almost tender, drain them and put them in a bowl.

2. Chop the onion, tomato, cucumber and herbs and add them to the lentils.

3. Add the lemon juice, and salt to taste. Mix well. Let the salad marinate for at least one hour, or if possible, three or more hours.

4. Serve on a small plate alone or with a little bread.

ENSALADA DE MANZANA Y NUECES

Apple and Walnut Salad

Ingredients

560 g of a mixture of red and green apples, chopped
280 g of chopped celery
250 g of chopped walnuts
130 g of raisins
130 ml of mayonnaise
Juice of half a lemon

Preparation

1. Mix all the ingredients and put them in a sealed container.

2. Refrigerate for several hours until chilled.

3. Serve the salad in small glass bowls with a little bread.

ENSALADA DE PASTA CON SALSA PESTO

Pasta Salad with Pesto Sauce

Ingredients:

> 400 g of macaroni (penne)
> 200 g of cherry tomatoes
> 150 g of rocket leaf
> 20 large fresh basil leaves
> 4 cloves of garlic
> 40 g of pine kernels
> 70 g of mature sheep' cheese, grated
> 100 ml of stoned olives (green or black)
> Olive oil
> Salt
> Ground black pepper

Preparation:

1. Cook the pasta until tender, drain and rinse.

2. Wash the rocket leaves and the basil leaves. Clean and cut the tomatoes into quarters. Mix the cooled pasta, tomatoes and rocket leaf together in a salad bowl and place it in the fridge.

3. To prepare the pesto: toast the pine kernels in a frying pan without any oil. Peel the garlic. Put the garlic into a large mortar with a little salt and crush into a puree. Add the basil and continue grinding until obtaining a smooth paste. Grind some of the toasted pine kernels and add them to the mixture. Keep some whole pine kernels aside for garnish. Add the grated cheese. Add olive oil and continue to grind and blend the mixture until smooth.

4. Serve the pasta salad in small bowls, topped with a spoonful of pesto and a slice of bread.

ENSALADA DE PIMIENTOS ASADOS

Grilled Pepper Salad

Ingredients:

>   2 red peppers
>   2 green or yellow peppers
>   1 or 2 ripe tomatoes
>   1 large onion
>   Vinegar (to taste)
>   Olive oil
>   Salt (to taste)

Preparation:

1. Roast the peppers together with the tomatoes. When they are roasted, place them in a sealed container to cool and release their juices.

2. Once cooled, peel the peppers, cut them into strips and put them in a bowl. Skin and mince the tomatoes and add to the peppers. Keep the juices from both.

3. Pour the juices from the peppers and tomatoes into a bowl, sieve them, and add a little seasoning, some vinegar, and a dash of olive oil. Stir the dressing into the salad and put the chopped onion on top.

ENSALADA DE PIMIENTOS DE PADRÓN Y QUESO FRESCO DE CABRA

Pepper Salad with Fresh Goats' Cheese

Ingredients:

>400 g of Padrón peppers
>200 g of fresh goats' cheese
>1 tablespoon of hazelnuts
>Olive oil
>100 ml of vinegar
>1 sprig of oregano
>1 sprig of thyme
>2 leaves of sage
>Pepper
>Salt

Preparation:

1. Cut the cheese into cubes and put these in a bowl along with the chopped herbs. Leave in the fridge to marinate for two hours.

2. Make a vinaigrette by toasting the hazelnuts in 20 ml of olive oil. Remove from the heat and mash them. Add vinegar, salt and pepper to taste.

3. Fry the peppers on both sides in a frying pan with olive oil. Remove and drain excess oil. Add salt to taste.

4. Mix the cheese with the Padrón peppers and serve the salad on small plates dressed with a little of the vinaigrette.

ENSALADILLA RUSA
Russian Salad

Despite the fact that this salad originated in 19th century Russia, we include it here because it has long been one of Spain's most popular tapas dishes. Very few bars anywhere in Spain will be without some variant of Russian salad.

Variations: You can also include celery, "reineta" apples and nuts which should be quite finely chopped. You can also make the salad with all mashed potato or all cubed potato if you prefer. Here we have a mixture of the two.

Ingredients:

> 500 g of mixed potatoes (1 firm variety, 1 purée variety)
> 1 large carrot, diced
> 125 g of French beans, chopped
> 125 g of peas
> 2 red peppers, chopped
> Garlic to your taste, chopped finely
> Mayonnaise or alioli
> A handful of green, stoned olives, chopped
> 3 gherkins, diced
> 2 teaspoons of capers
> 2 hard-boiled eggs, roughly chopped

Preparation:

1. Peel and boil the potatoes for puréeing. Mash them.

2. Scrape the firm variety of potatoes, cut them into smallish dices, and boil these until tender.

3. Boil or steam the carrot, beans, peas and peppers until just tender - don't overcook them.

4. Mix both types of potato with the cooked vegetables and the garlic in a bowl.

5. Add a liberal amount of mayonnaise or alioli. Mix thoroughly.

6. Gently stir in the olives, capers and gherkins. Place in the fridge to cool completely. Serve in small dishes and garnish as desired with some chopped egg and a few bread sticks.

ENSALADA TEMPLADA DE ALUBIAS Y CALABAZA.

Warm Bean and Pumpkin Salad

"Warm salads" might sound like a contradiction to non-Mediterranean cooks but there are many such warm salads in the Spanish cuisine - where several of the ingredients are cooked and served hot together with traditional cold salad ingredients. It is a surprisingly pleasant combination.

Ingredients:

> 200 g of pumpkin
> 50 g of rocket leaf
> 200 g of cooked white kidney beans
> 10 g of pumpkin seeds
> 3 tablespoons of vegetable broth
> 3 tablespoons of olive oil
> 1 teaspoon of mustard
> Salt
> Pepper

Preparation:

1. Wash the pumpkin, and without removing the skin, chop it into cubes of about 1 centimetre. Sauté the pumpkin in a frying pan with 1 tablespoon of olive oil over a medium heat for about 12 minutes. Once the pumpkin is tender, season with salt and pepper.

2. Make the dressing: Chop half of the rocket leaf very finely. Mix this together with the mustard, 2 tablespoons of olive oil, pumpkin seeds, and the warm vegetable stock. Stir until slightly emulsified. Add salt to taste and set aside.

3. Strain and rinse the cooked beans. Let them drain and then mix them with the dressing. Stir well, being careful not to break the beans.

4. Put the remaining rocket leaves as a base in individual small bowls. Place the white beans with the dressing on top of these. Finally, finish off with the warm pumpkin and serve immediately.

ESCALIVADA

Pepper and Aubergine Salad

This is an old Catalan roast pepper and aubergine salad. Escalivada means "cooked in hot ashes", which is the traditional way to roast vegetables Nowadays, of course, we use a grill. This makes an excellent tapa or starter. You can use any additional grilled or roasted vegetables you like, especially tomatoes and onions.

Ingredients:

      125 ml of olive oil
      Garlic, crushed
      4 sweet red peppers
      4 aubergines
      Salt
      Tomatoes (optional)
      Onions (optional)
      Parsley, finely chopped

Preparation:

1. Grill the peppers and aubergines (and optionally onions and tomatoes) whole in the oven for about 25 minutes or until the skins start to blacken. Peel them and let them cool.

2. Remove the seeds from the peppers and tomatoes and cut all the vegetables into strips. Place these strips in a bowl and sprinkle with a little salt.

3. Dress the vegetables with olive oil seasoned with crushed garlic.

4. Serve the roasted vegetables sprinkled with fresh parsley on a slice of crusty bread.

PEPINOS ALIÑADOS

Cucumber Pickles

Pickles are quite popular in Spain and are often served as tapas, sometimes with a little bread or on skewers with other pickles, roasted peppers and olives.

Ingredients:

> 5 small cucumbers
> Salt
> 4 tablespoons of wine vinegar
> 1 tablespoon of sugar (white or brown)
> 3 scallions, coarsely chopped (or a chopped onion)
> Half a teaspoon of hot chilli pepper flakes (to your taste)
> 2-3 tablespoons of warm water

Preparation:

1. Wash the cucumbers. Slice them fairly thin (about 0.25 cm). Put them in a bowl and cover with a sprinkling of salt. Toss until all cucumber slices are coated.

2. Place the slices in a colander and allow the water and salt to drain from the cucumber for about 30 minutes.

3. Meanwhile, make the marinade by mixing the vinegar, sugar, and water until the sugar dissolves. Stir in the chilli pepper and onion.

4. When the cucumbers have drained, squeeze them by hand over the sink to remove excess water. Place them in a bowl and add the marinade mixture. Toss well.

5. They can be eaten immediately, but will keep in the fridge for a few days.

PIPIRRANA

Mixed Salad

Pipirrana is a refreshing and nutritious salad, very tasty, easy and quick to prepare. Many local dishes don't have a strict method of preparation or an exact list of ingredients. They developed over time and many variants evolved throughout the years. As popular dishes, families and villages have made them with whatever ingredients were affordable or seasonal. Pipirrana is a typical example of one of these ad-hoc dishes. Basically, it is a salad prepared with whatever fresh salad vegetables you have.

Ingredients:

> 1 cucumber
> 1 green pepper
> Half a sweet red pepper
> 2 ripe tomatoes
> 2 cloves of garlic
> Half an onion
> Marinated olives
> 3 bread slices
> 2 tablespoons of olive oil
> 2 tablespoons of wine vinegar
>
> Salt and Black pepper

Preparation:

1. Wash the peppers, remove the seeds, and chop into small cubes.

2. Peel and dice the cucumber and tomatoes. Chop the garlic and onion very finely.

3. Mix all the vegetables and dress with the vinegar, oil, pepper and salt, or prepare a vinaigrette with these ingredients, leave it to stand for an hour and then dress.

4. Chop the olives into very small pieces and sprinkle them on the salad.Refrigerate for half an hour before serving. Serve with bread.

REMOLACHAS ALIÑÁS A LA SEVILLANA

Beetroot in Vinegar of Sevilla

This is a typical Sevilla dish, served during the great heat of mid summer, either as a salad tapa or to accompany another dish.

Ingredients:

> 2 bunches of fresh beetroot
> 2 onions
> 1 big sprig of fresh parsley
> Salt
> Olive oil
> White wine vinegar

Preparation:

1. Boil the beetroot in a saucepan with a pinch of salt and a dash of vinegar until they are tender.

2. Remove from the heat, drain and let them cool. Peel and slice.

3. Peel the onions and cut them into thin slices. Finely chop the parsley.

4. Put the beetroot in a bowl and cover with the onion and parsley.

5. Season to taste with oil, vinegar and salt.

6. Serve cold in small bowls with a slice of bread.

TOMATES ALIÑADOS

Tomatoes in Garlic Dressing

This is a very simple but popular tapa in many parts of Spain. It is a very pleasant and refreshing dish, especially in the summer. You can also use basil and/or thyme as a herbal seasoning.

Ingredients:

>Several ripe tomatoes
>Garlic
>Salt, to taste
>Olive oil
>Vinegar
>Oregano, to taste

Preparation:

1. Wash the tomatoes, cut them into slices and lay out the slices on a tray.

2. Crush some garlic with salt and oregano in a mortar and pestle.

3. Take a little vinegar and olive oil (1 to 3 approximately) and, little by little, add these to the herb mixture, beating with a fork. Add the oil and vinegar slowly so as to form a more or less uniform sauce.

4. Finally, with a spoon, dress the tomato slices with some of this garlic and herb sauce.

5. Serve as a tapa by itself or with a little bread.

ZANAHORÍAS ALIÑADAS

Marinated Carrots

Ingredients:

> 6-7 large carrots
> 4 garlic cloves
> 1 tablespoon of dried oregano
> 2 teaspoons of cumin
> 1 teaspoon of paprika powder (sweet or hot)
> 65 ml of vinegar of Jerez
> 65 ml of water
> 2-3 sprigs of parsley, finely chopped
> Salt to taste
> Olive oil

Preparation:

1. Clean the carrots. Boil them whole until tender, but still crisp. Take them out of the pan, and leave them to cool in cold water.

2. Peel the garlic. Place the garlic and the spices into a mortar together with a tablespoon of water and crush everything into a paste, adding a bit more water if needed.

3. Cut the carrots into thick slices and place them into a dish. Add the spice mixture. Pour the vinegar and water into the dish until the carrots are covered. If more liquid is needed to cover the carrots, add equal parts of vinegar and water.

4. Refrigerate the marinade for at least 4 hours, but preferably overnight.

5. When they are ready to serve, remove the carrots from the marinade and drain. Place them in a serving dish. Sprinkle with the chopped parsley and add a little olive oil. Serve with slices of baguette or cateto bread.

---oOo---

2.11 Vegetable Tapas

AGUACATE CON QUESO DE CABRA
Avocado with Fresh Goats' Cheese

Ingredients:

> Avocados
> A roll of fresh goats' cheese (Rulo de cabra)
> Molasses
> Olive oil
> Salt

Preparation:

1. Peel the avocados and cut them into thick slices. Arrange the slices on plates in a fan shape from the centre out.

2. Cut the roll of cheese into thick slices (1.5 cm) and sear these in a non-stick frying pan for a few moments, then place the hot cheese in the centre of each plate.

3. Season with a little salt, a drop of molasses and some olive oil. Serve immediately with a slice of bread.

AGUACATES RELLENOS

Filled Avocados

Avocados are especially suitable to create delicious filled tapas when the stone is removed. Here are some ideas for fillings:

> Cream cheese with walnut
> Fresh goats' cheese
> Finely chopped salad (like a Pipirrana salad)
> Russian salad
> Olive tapenade
> Lentil salad
> Rice salad
> Sprouted beans

Preparation:

1. Simply cut the avocado in half lengthways and remove the stone.

2. Fill the cavity left by the stone with your chosen filling and serve as a tapa.

ALCACHOFAS REBOZADAS

Fried Artichokes

Ingredients:

> Half a litre of water
> Lemon juice
> 4 small-artichokes
> 2 eggs
> 60 g of flour (wheat or chickpea flour)
> Salt
> Alioli sauce (see recipe under sauces)
> Olive oil

Preparation:

1. Pour water into a mixing bowl and add the juice from half a lemon.

2. Remove the outer leaves from the artichokes. Cut off the stalk and the tops of the leaves. Cut the artichokes into quarters and place them in the bowl of water and lemon juice.

3. Pour 300 ml of olive oil into a large frying pan on medium-high heat.

4. Shake the flour onto a large plate, add a pinch of salt, and mix. Beat the two eggs in a small bowl.

5. When the oil is almost hot, remove the cut artichoke quarters from the water and drain thoroughly. Coat the artichokes with flour and then dip them into the beaten egg. Immediately place them into the hot oil. Fry on both sides until golden brown.

6. Remove them from the oil and allow them to drain on paper towels.

7. Serve hot with an alioli sauce.

ASADILLO DE LA MANCHA

Pepper Casserole of La Mancha

The asadillo de la Mancha (also known as asadillo manchego) is a traditional dish whose main ingredient is roasted red pepper, baked in a clay bowl. This is a simple recipe, characteristic of La Mancha, which uses local products. This tapa is served in the same clay pot in which it is cooked.

Ingredients:

> 6 tablespoons of olive oil
> Garlic to taste, chopped
> 4 large sweet red peppers, roasted, skins and seeds removed and cut into strips
> 4 large, firm tomatoes, sliced
> 2 teaspoons of oregano
> Salt and Pepper

Preparation:

1. You can prepare your own roasted red peppers but they are readily available in jars, already prepared. The best quality and most typical peppers for this dish are the "Pimientos del Piquillo de Lodosa", but these peppers are small, so you will need to adjust the number you use.

2. Pre-heat the oven to 230°C. Grease a shallow baking dish or casserole with some of the oil.

3. Using a little more oil, gently sauté the garlic until barely golden. Keep the oil.

4. Arrange a layer of peppers in the bottom of the baking dish.

5. Sprinkle some of the garlic over the peppers and follow this with a layer of tomatoes, seasoning between the layers with salt and pepper.

6. Continue layering until you have used up all the ingredients.

7. Pour the remaining oil and the oil in which you sautéed the garlic over the vegetables and sprinkle with the oregano. Bake for about 20-25 minutes. Serve with a slice of bread in the same bowl. Asadillo can be served hot or cold and is sometimes accompanied with slices of hardboiled egg.

BERENJENAS CON MIEL DE CAÑA

Aubergine with Molasses

The preparation of aubergines cut into thin slices, battered, fried and decorated with some drops of thick, sweet molasses has become a very popular dish in recent years. It now appears as an option on the menu of many restaurants throughout Andalucía. It is often served as a tapa, but can also be part of a main course or even a sweet.

Ingredients:

> 2 large aubergines
> 1 bottle of beer
> Flour
> 1 egg white
> Yeast (the tip of a teaspoon)
> Molasses (to taste)
> Olive oil
> Salt (to taste)

Preparation:

1. Make a batter in a bowl by whisking an egg white until stiff and then fold in the flour, salt and yeast. Then gradually pour in the beer whilst mixing until you have a quite thick batter mix (it should be like a thick soup and should not have any lumps).

2. Wash the aubergines, cut them across in slices of about 1 centimetre thick with the skin and then cut these in half so you have a lot of semi-circles of aubergine.

3. Dip the half slices of aubergine into the batter and then fry them in a pan with very hot oil (or, to make them even crispier, in a deep fat fryer).

4. Once browned, take them out and let them drain on a paper towel. Serve hot with a little molasses poured over them.

BERENJENA REBOZADA

Aubergine Fritters

Ingredients

> 1 aubergine
> 3 eggs
> 200 g of wheat flour
> 1 sachet of dried yeast
> Salt
> Water
> Olive oil

Preparation:

1. Wash the aubergine and cut it into thin slices.

2. Place the slices in a bowl and cover them with water and a little salt. Let them soak for at least 12 hours.

3. When you are ready to make the fritters, whisk the eggs together thoroughly in a bowl. Add the yeast whilst beating. Add the flour little by little, stirring constantly. The texture of the dough has to be something like a smooth porridge, so if it is too thick then add a little water.

4. Put the well-drained aubergine slices in the bowl with batter, coating them evenly

5. Put plenty of oil into a pan and put it on a medium heat.

6. When the oil is hot, add the slices of battered aubergine.

7. When the slices start to brown on one side turn them over until they are golden brown on both sides.

8. Put the fritters on kitchen paper to drain the excess oil.

9. Serve hot on a small plate with a little salt.

CALABACÍN A LA VINAGRETA

Courgette in Vinaigrette

Ingredients:

> Courgette
> Olive oil
> Vinegar
> Garlic
> Parsley
> Salt

Preparation:

1. Wash and peel the courgette and cut it into thin strips, not very long.

2. Crush 2 cloves of garlic and a small handful of parsley in a mortar.

3. Make the vinaigrette with oil and vinegar, with a ratio of 3 parts of oil to one of vinegar. Add the garlic and parsley paste and stir until blended, adding a little salt.

4. Place the courgette strips in a bowl and sprinkle with the vinaigrette. Mix well; cover the bowl and leave to marinade in the fridge overnight.

5. Serve as a tapa by itself or use the strips as an ingredient in other tapas; for instance, to roll-up with cream cheese or other fillings.

CALABAZA FRITA DE MÁLAGA

Fried Pumpkin of Málaga

This is one of the most distinctive dishes of the villages of Málaga province and makes a delicious appetizer.

Ingredients:

> 300 g of peeled pumpkin
> 100 g of old bread (cateto)
> 3 cloves of garlic
> 2 tablespoons of sherry vinegar
> 3 tablespoons of olive oil
> Oregano
> Parsley
> Salt

Preparation:

1. Make a majado: Put a little salt with the garlic cloves in a mortar and grind them to a paste.

2. Toast the bread, dip it in vinegar and add this to the garlic paste; continue mashing these together.

3. Add finely chopped oregano and parsley.

4. The mixture is ready when it has a smooth, uniform consistency.

5. Chop up the pumpkin and sauté it in a frying pan with olive oil over a high heat.

6. When the pumpkin begins to brown, reduce the heat and add the majado.

7. Cook this over a medium heat for about 10 minutes, stirring constantly.

8. Serve it, either hot or cold, on some freshly toasted bread.

CAZUELA DE HABAS

Broad Bean Casserole

Broad beans have a long and mystical history ranging back to ancient Egypt, and they became very popular in Roman times, spreading throughout the empire in their dry form for food or cultivation. Today, few small farms in Spain would be without their patch of broad beans. They have excellent nutritional qualities and their strong taste makes them a favourite in many dishes.

Here, we have a simple traditional tapa based on dried beans that is still popular throughout Spain today.

Ingredients:

>   0.5 kg of dried broad beans
>   1 onion
>   2 cloves of garlic
>   3 small chillies
>   Half a red pepper (chopped finely)
>   Paprika powder, sweet and / or hot
>   1 bay leaf
>   Oregano
>   Parsley
>   Raw almonds flakes
>   3 tablespoons of olive oil
>   Salt
>   1 litre of water (or more if required)

Preparation:

1. The night before you need them, put the beans in a bowl and cover them with water to soak and re-hydrate them for between 12 and 18 hours. Drain the beans before cooking them.

2. Peel and chop the onion and the garlic and wash and chop the chillies.

3. Sauté those in a large casserole dish.

3. Add the red pepper and the paprika powder and mix well. Pour half a litre of water into the casserole and a little olive oil. Add the beans. (From now on, every time you need to add water you should use only boiling water so as not to interrupt the cooking process.)

5. When the vegetables start to boil, add the bay leaf, oregano and parsley.

6. Cover and cook over a medium heat for about 45 min. Keep an eye on the dish in case you need to add some boiling water as required.

7. Add salt to taste, as well as the sliced almonds and then continue cooking for 15-20 min. more.

8. When the beans are tender, serve hot in small separate earthenware bowls.

CHIPS DE VERDURAS

Vegetable Crisps

This is a tasty and interesting way of making crispy fried vegetables.

Ingredients:

> 1 raw beetroot
> 1 large potato
> 1 large carrot
> Salt
> Olive oil
> Half a teaspoon of spices (cloves, cinnamon, pepper and nutmeg)

Preparation:

1. Wash, dry and peel all the vegetables.

2. Cut the carrots, potatoes and beetroot into thin slices. Remember they should be like potato crisps when cooked - so they need to be thin.

3. Fry the vegetables in a pan with hot olive oil until golden and crisp.

4. Remove the vegetable slices from the pan and let them drain on paper kitchen towels.

5. Grind the spices with the coarse salt in a mortar and pestle and sprinkle this mix on the crisps.

6. Serve warm.

COLES MOREÁS

Golden Fried Cabbage

This is a simple favourite dish in Málaga in Andalucía where it is often served as a tapa with a slice of bread.

Ingredients:

>   1 cabbage
>   4 tablespoons of olive oil
>   3 cloves of garlic
>   1 tablespoon of sweet paprika powder
>   Salt

Preparation:

1. Chop the cabbage.

2. Toast the garlic with some olive oil in a frying pan.

3. When the garlic has browned, add a tablespoon of paprika powder, stir, and quickly add the chopped cabbage and a little salt.

4. Stir well and cook until the cabbage is tender, which takes about 30 minutes.

5. Serve hot alone or with a slice of bread.

COLIFLOR REBOZADA

Cauliflower Fritters

This recipe almost certainly uses cauliflower as a substitute for cod. Even though cod was long considered food for the poor, many couldn't even afford cod, but they still made the same "tortillas", substituting the cod for chunks of cauliflower with extraordinary and very tasty results. This is also known in some parts of Spain as Tortillitas de Coliflor. This particular version of the recipe comes from the province of Badajoz in Extremadura. It is served as a tapa with alioli sauce.

Ingredients:

> 0.5 kg of cauliflower
> 2 eggs
> 2 cloves of garlic
> 1 large sprig of parsley
> Flour
> Vinegar
> Olive oil
> Salt (to taste)
> Alioli sauce (see recipe under "sauces")

Preparation:

1. Clean the cauliflower. Place the florets in a bowl, sprinkle with salt, parsley and a dash of vinegar. Let the florets marinate for at least 3 hours.

2. Boil the cauliflower in salted water until it is tender. Drain it and allow it to cool.

3. Beat the eggs and crumbled pieces of cauliflower in a bowl. Finely chop and add the parsley and garlic. Add salt to taste. Add the flour little by little, stirring with a wooden spoon until the mix thickens slightly.

4. Put plenty of oil in a pan and heat it. When the oil is hot spoon portions of the cauliflower mixture into the hot oil and fry.

5. When the tortillas are golden brown, take them out and put them on kitchen paper to drain the excess oil. The dish can be made by separating the cauliflower into florets, coating them in batter and deep-frying them. Sprinkle with fresh parsley and serve one or two florets on a small plate with some alioli sauce.

ESPINACAS A LA CATALANA

Catalan Spinach with Currants and Pine kernels

This is a very simple, classic Catalan recipe for steamed spinach.

The recipe is very similar to the "Espinacas Sacromonte", which is a traditional dish from the Gypsy district of Granada. The only difference between the recipes is that the Granada recipe adds a splash of wine vinegar and uses fresh almonds instead of pine kernels.

Ingredients:

> 2 bunches of fresh spinach
> 2 cloves of garlic
> 3 tablespoons of pine kernels
> 3 tablespoons of currants or raisins
> Olive oil
> 4 slices of dry white bread

Preparation:

1. Wash the spinach thoroughly and trim off the stems. Steam the spinach for only 2-3 minutes. Remove from the pan immediately and allow it to drain well.

2. Peel and slice the garlic. Pour a few tablespoons of olive oil to cover the bottom of a large frying pan. Fry the garlic for about 2 minutes.

3. Add the currants or raisins and pine kernels to the pan and continue to sauté for 1 minute.

4. Add the drained spinach to the pan and mix well, coating all ingredients with oil.

5. Add a little salt to your taste.

6. Lightly toast the slices of bread, cut in them quarters.

7. Serve the spinach with the slices of toast.

ESPINACAS Y GARBANZOS

Spinach and Chickpeas

This is another version of the popular combination of chickpeas and spinach as a tapa.

Ingredients:

> 6 tablespoons of olive oil
> 3 slices of white bread, crusts removed, diced
> 3 cloves of garlic, thinly sliced
> 1 teaspoon of ground cumin
> 1 tablespoon of red wine or sherry vinegar
> 800 g of cooked chickpeas, rinsed and drained
> 450 g of fresh spinach
> Freshly ground black pepper
> Salt

Preparation:

1. Heat the olive oil in a large frying pan over a medium heat.

2. Add the bread cubes and fry them for 5 minutes until golden brown on all sides. Add the garlic and cumin and cook for 1-2 minutes, until the garlic begins to brown.

3. Transfer to a mortar and pestle or a food processor. Add the vinegar and blend or process to a paste.

4. Return the bread paste to the pan and add the drained chick peas.

5. Cook, stirring, until the chick peas have absorbed the flavours and are hot, then season with salt and freshly ground pepper. If the consistency is a little thick, add some water. Now add the spinach and cook until just wilted, about 2 minutes. Correct the salt and pepper, if necessary.

6. Serve hot in small bowls with a little toast. Optionally, add a slice of boiled egg.

FRITURA DE BERENJENA Y CALABACÍN

Aubergine and Courgette Fritters

Ingredients:

> 1 large aubergine
> 1 large courgette
> 1 small bottle of lager
> Salt and freshly ground pepper
> Olive oil
> Pastry flour

Preparation:

1. Cut the aubergine into sticks, like French fries but thicker. Scatter some salt on them and let them stand for half an hour to release their juice. This is important because they will be crispier when fried.

2. Meanwhile cut the courgette in the same way.

3. When the aubergines are ready, put them with the courgette chips and sprinkle them all with the beer. Let the chips rest in the beer for at least 15 minutes.

4. Drain the liquid off and then coat the chips with flour, making sure to cover them all evenly.

5. Now fry the aubergine and courgette in hot olive oil. When they are golden brown, remove the chips from the oil and drain quickly. They must be served hot and crispy.

6. Serve the fritters on a small plate with hot tomato sauce, salsa romesco or homemade gazpacho.

HABAS ENZAPATÁS

Broad Beans Enzapatás

Enzapatás is a typical broad bean dish from the province of Huelva (and the Portuguese Algarve). In many areas the dish is prepared with pennyroyal instead of coriander, or a mixture of both. You can also add some mint leaves.

As a tapa it can be served hot or cold.

Ingredients:

> 0.5 kg of large fresh broad beans
> 5 chopped garlic cloves
> 2 whole garlic cloves
> Fresh coriander (and pennyroyal / mint)
> Salt
> A few drops of lemon juice

Preparation:

1. Put the beans and garlic in water, and boil until tender (about 20 minutes).

2. Season generously, using plenty of coriander (and/or pennyroyal and mint) to your taste, lemon juice and a little salt.

3. Serve the beans hot or cold in small bowls with a slice of toasted bread.

MORRETE CALIENTE

Mushroom and Asparagus Casserole

Although it is quite common to use green asparagus these days, this traditional dish of Andalucía was born out of poverty, using wild mushrooms, thistles and wild asparagus. The remaining ingredients in this casserole are the usual components of popular cuisine: bread, almonds and garlic. Despite their origins in very hard times, cardo thistles and wild asparagus are now considered delicacies.

Ingredients:

> 200 g of cardo thistles (cardoons)
> 200 g of green asparagus
> 200 g of oyster mushrooms
> 200 g of almonds
> 2 cloves of garlic
> 1 slice of "cateto" bread
> Olive oil
> Salt (to taste)
> Vinegar

Preparation:

1. Fry the bread (first soaked in some water), the almonds and garlic, and make a majaíllo with these ingredients.

2. Separately (because of different cooking times) cook and season the chopped cardoons, the asparagus and the mushrooms, until each is tender.

3. Once cooked, mix and sauté the cardoons, asparagus and mushrooms together in a little olive oil and add the majaíllo with a drop of water.

4. Leave the dish to simmer for about 15 minutes until it is thick and savoury.

5. Season and serve hot. It is common to add a few drops of vinegar.

MORRETE CALIENTE DE MÁLAGA

Mushroom and Potato Casserole of Málaga

This dish is typical of rural Málaga, which is well-known for the variety of wild mushrooms that are to be found in the area in the autumn and winter.

Ingredients:

> 1 kg of potatoes
> 0.5 kg of mushrooms, e.g. oyster mushrooms
> Dry breadcrumbs (previous day's bread)
> 1 clove of garlic
> Strands of saffron
> Ground pepper
> Paprika (a pinch)
> Water
> Vinegar

Preparation:

1. Cut the potatoes and mushrooms into chunks, fry them separately and drain off the oil.

2. Put the garlic, saffron, paprika, breadcrumbs, water and a little vinegar in a blender. Blend well to a thick paste.

3. Put the potatoes in a frying pan or heatproof casserole dish without oil, and put the mushrooms on top of them. Add the paste that you made in the blender and any extra seasoning to taste.

4. If it looks too thick, add a little more water.

5. Cook for 4 to 5 minutes, but don't let it get too thick. Serve hot.

PARPUCHAS DE ESPÁRRAGOS DE ANDALUCÍA

Asparagus Pancakes of Andalucía

Ingredients:

1 kg of asparagus
Flour
1 egg
Salt
Garlic
Water
Yeast
Parsley
Olive oil
Molasses

Preparation:

1. Chop the asparagus and cook them for 20 minutes in boiling water.

2. In a bowl, beat the egg, adding the chopped garlic, parsley, salt, water, yeast and flour until the dough thickens.

3. Mix the drained asparagus in with the dough.

4. Fry spoonfuls of the dough in a frying pan with olive oil.

5. Serve hot with molasses.

PATATAS RELLENAS DE ESPINACAS Y PIÑONES

Potatoes Stuffed with Spinach and Pine kernels

Ingredients:

> 4 large potatoes
> 1 kg of fresh spinach
> 250 g of pumpkin
> 50 g of rice
> 4 thin slices of semi-mature goats' cheese
> 1 handful of pine kernels
> 2 cloves of garlic
> Water
> Olive oil
> Salt
> Parsley

Preparation:

1. Thoroughly clean the potatoes and cook them in a saucepan with water and a pinch of salt. Cook them for about 30 minutes. They should remain whole.

2. Cut the potatoes in half - lengthways. Scoop out the potato and mash it to a puree with a fork.

3. Thoroughly clean the spinach.

4. Peel the pumpkin and cut it into cubes. Cook the pumpkin along with the rice in a saucepan with water and salt for 18 minutes.

5. Chop the cloves of garlic and fry them in some olive oil. When they start to brown, add the pine kernels until they are toasted. Add the spinach and when fried a little, add the mashed potato and stir together well.

6. Fill the empty potato skins with the spinach-potato mixture and put a slice of cheese on top. Bake at 180ºC for 6-8 minutes.

7. Blend the pumpkin into a very smooth cream.

8. When the cheese is melted, serve a stuffed potato hot on a small plate with the pumpkin cream as a base. Garnish with a sprig of fresh parsley.

PIMIENTOS FRITOS CON CEBOLLA

Fried Peppers with Onion

This is a simple recipe for fried vegetables which is a great favourite in all of Spain, but especially in Andalucía. You can also add strips of aubergine, courgette or asparagus to make the tapa more interesting.

Ingredients:

> 4 large peppers (red, green, yellow)
> 1 large onion
> Olive oil
> Salt to taste

Preparation:

1. Clean the peppers and remove the stems and seeds. Cut them lengthwise into thin strips (about 0.2cm).

2. Peel and cut the onion into thin slices.

3. Pour 4-5 tablespoons of olive oil into a frying pan and fry the pepper strips, stirring often.

4. When the peppers begin to soften, add the onion slices and continue to fry.

5. Add salt to taste.

6. Remove the vegetable mix from the pan when the onions soften and become translucent.

7. Serve hot on a slice of cateto bread.

PIMIENTOS DE PADRÓN FRITOS

Fried Padrón Peppers

The tiny "padrón" peppers from Galicia are fried and sprinkled with coarse salt. A simple and easy tapa recipe that is popular all over Spain.

Ingredients:

> 300-500 g of fresh padrón peppers
> 0.5 litre of olive oil
> Coarse salt

Preparation:

1. Wash the peppers under cold water and dry them thoroughly. Leave the stems on the peppers.

2. Pour the olive oil into a frying pan and put the pan on a medium heat. (You can optionally add some crushed garlic here, but traditionally the peppers are fried without garlic).

3. When the olive oil is hot, place some of the peppers (whole) into the pan and fry for 2-3 minutes, making sure to cook them on both sides. Continue to fry the peppers in batches and let them drain on paper towels.

4. Sprinkle the fried peppers with a little coarse salt and serve warm.

PIMIENTO DEL PIQUILLO

Piquillo Peppers

This is a very simple and popular tapa made with piquillo peppers and garlic. Piquillo peppers are produced and preserved in large quantities in Spain. You can roast and skin any fresh red peppers, but the piquillo peppers are of an excellent quality and have a particularly sweet taste. It is therefore perhaps easier to simply buy the preserved roasted piquillo peppers ready for use. There are many recipes for stuffed piquillo peppers, but they are delicious as they are.

Ingredients:

> 12 roasted piquillo peppers
> 2 cloves of garlic
> Sherry vinegar
> Olive oil

Preparation:

1. Drain the whole piquillo peppers and arrange them around a plate.

2. Peel and mince the garlic cloves. Place it in a small bowl and add a few tablespoons each of vinegar and oil. Whisk and pour the mixture over the peppers.

3. Serve with slices of cateto or similar country bread.

PIMIENTO DEL PIQUILLO RELLENO DE QUESO DE CABRA FRESCO

Piquillo Peppers filled with Fresh Goats' Cheese

Piquillo peppers are most often bought in jars or tins, preserved in olive oil. They are very popular as a tapa and can be filled with a lot of different ingredients. They have a very characteristic sweet flavour. In this recipe they are filled with fresh goats' cheese and served cold.

Ingredients:

> 1 tin or jar of preserved whole piquillo peppers
> Fresh, creamy goats' cheese
> 1 clove of garlic, finely chopped
> Fresh parsley, finely chopped
> Salt
> Pepper

Preparation:

1. Mix the chopped garlic and parsley with the goats' cheese, season it with salt and pepper and fill the peppers with the mixture.

2. Serve each pepper on a small plate on a bed of lettuce or with a little salmorejo sauce.

PIMIENTOS DEL PIQUILLO RELLENOS DE SETAS Y ESPINACAS

Piquillo Peppers Stuffed with Mushroom and Spinach

Ingredients:

> 300 g of piquillo peppers (about 12)
> 225 g of frozen spinach (or cooked fresh, weight after draining)
> 300 g of fresh mushrooms
> 2 cloves of garlic
> Olive oil
> Béchamel Sauce:
> 250 ml of milk
> 50 g of butter
> 50 g of flour
> Salt and pepper to taste

Preparation:

1. Prepare the filling: Cook the spinach and ensure that it is as well-drained as possible.

2. Clean the mushrooms. Chop them into small pieces (of about 1 cm) and set aside. Peel and cut the cloves of garlic lengthwise into thin slices.

3. Sauté the garlic in olive oil, but don't let it brown. Add the mushrooms and continue to cook, stirring occasionally. Finally, add the drained spinach and mix thoroughly. Add salt and pepper to taste. Set aside when the mushrooms are tender.

4. Prepare the béchamel sauce: heat the milk in a small sauce pan until it is warm, but do not bring it to a boil. Melt the butter in a small frying pan. Add the flour and fry briefly, stirring constantly. Slowly pour in the warm milk whilst continuing to stir, until the flour has been completely absorbed by the milk, and the mixture begins to thicken into a sauce. Add some salt to taste. Remove from the heat.

5. Stir some of the béchamel sauce into the mushroom-spinach mix and blend together. Carefully fill each of the peppers, using a small spoon.

6. Place the peppers with a little béchamel over each pepper on individual heatproof earthenware plates and briefly place these under the grill to gratinate the béchamel. Serve hot with a slice of bread.

PIMIENTOS VERDES RELLENOS DE TORTILLA DE PATATAS

Green Peppers Filled with Tortilla

This popular tapa dish combines two Spanish culinary favourites: tortilla and peppers. The green peppers used are the long green "frying" peppers, but you can also use the long red peppers which are seasonally available.

Ingredients:

> 3 or 4 medium potatoes, peeled
> 1 onion
> 3 eggs
> 1 teaspoon of salt
> 5 or 6 long green peppers (or a mixture of long green and long red peppers)
> Olive oil for frying
> 1 baguette, sliced

Preparation:

1. Cut the peeled potatoes into 1 cm cubes.

2. Peel and chop the onion. Put the potatoes and onions into a bowl and mix them together. Salt the mixture.

3. Heat the olive oil in a large frying pan on medium-high heat. Put the potato and onion mixture into the frying pan, spreading it out evenly. The oil should almost cover the potatoes. Turn down the heat slightly, so the potatoes cook inside and out, but do not burn.

4. Cut off the tops of the green peppers and remove as much of the inside as possible, being careful not to tear the side of the peppers. Set aside.

5. When the potatoes are tender, remove them from the pan and put them in a colander to allow oil to drain off.

6. Meanwhile, beat the eggs in a mixing bowl. Stir in the potato-onion mixture.

7. Spoon this mixture into the peppers, lightly pushing it down. Seal the end of each pepper with a little flour to keep the mixture in.

8. You can either fry the peppers or bake them. Traditionally they would be fried, but baking is a lower-fat option.

9. Frying: Heat about 1 cm of olive oil in a frying pan. Fry the peppers in the oil on a medium heat for about 6-10 minutes. Turn to cook on both sides. Remove and drain on a paper towel.

10. Baking: Instead of frying the peppers, bake them in a preheated oven at 180°C for about 15-20 minutes.

11. Cut the baguette into slices. When they are cool enough to touch, cut the peppers into pieces of about 5 cm thick and serve them on a slice of baguette

PINCHO VEGETAL

Mixed Vegetable Pinchos

Here is a basic recipe for a mixed vegetable pincho. There are many variations on this type of skewered vegetable tapa.

Ingredients:

1 large aubergine
1 courgette
1 spring onion
1 carrot
1 green pepper
4 cherry tomatoes
4 mushrooms
1 potato
Olive oil
A pinch of sugar
Salt
Pepper

Preparation:

1. Wash the vegetables and cut the aubergine and courgette into slices of about half a centimetre thick.

2. Peel the potato and cut it also into slices of about half a centimetre thick. Cut the de-seeded pepper into 4 parts.

3. Rub a baking dish with some olive oil and place the slices of vegetables in the dish. Season and put into a pre-heated (200°C) oven for 15 minutes or until the vegetables are tender.

4. Meanwhile, peel the carrot and the spring onion. Grate the carrot and cut the spring onion into very thin slices. Put a few drops of olive oil in a saucepan on a medium heat and put the carrots and spring onions into the pan. Stir in a pinch of sugar and salt, cover the pan and let the mixture simmer for about ten minutes.

5. Sauté the mushrooms in a pan with salt and pepper for a couple of minutes. Then remove and put aside.

6. When the vegetables are tender, take them from the oven and make up 4 wooden skewers as follows: First put a slice of aubergine, then courgette, then another aubergine, a slice of potato, the mushroom and

a strip of green pepper. Finish off with a cherry tomato on top of each skewer.

7. Sprinkle each skewer with a tablespoon of carrot and onion and a few drops of olive oil. Serve warm.

TOMATE AL HORNO CON AJO Y TOMILLO
Baked Tomato with Garlic and Thyme

This is a very fast and simple tapa with an appetizing aromatic smell.

Ingredients:

> 4 large tomatoes
> Olive oil
> Salt & pepper
> 4 cloves of garlic
> A few sprigs of thyme

Preparation:

1. Cut the top off the tomatoes, just enough to remove the stem.

2. Place the tomatoes in a small baking dish, with a drop of olive oil and seasoned with pepper and salt.

3. Insert a whole clove of garlic into each tomato. Chop and sprinkle half of the thyme on top of the tomatoes and place the dish in an oven pre-heated to 200°C for about 20 minutes.

4. When the tomatoes are cooked, sprinkle them with the rest of the fresh thyme.

5. Serve each tomato as a tapa with a piece of fresh baguette.

TOMATES REBOZADOS

Breaded Tomatoes

Ingredients:

 4 tomatoes
 4 eggs
 200 g of breadcrumbs
 100 g of flour
 1 tablespoon of basil (chopped or ground)
 Olive oil
 Pepper
 Salt

Preparation:

1. Wash and cut the tomatoes into thick slices. Season them.

2. Mix the basil with the breadcrumbs.

3. Beat the eggs in a bowl.

4. Dry the tomatoes. Pass the tomato slices through the flour, the egg and the breadcrumbs (in this order).

5. Fry in enough oil (or use a deep fryer) until golden.

6. Place on a paper towel to remove excess oil and serve hot.

TOMATES RELLENOS CON AJO Y PEREJIL

Tomatoes Filled with Garlic and Parsley

Ingredients:

> 2 large or 4 small tomatoes
> 2 cloves of garlic
> 50 g of breadcrumbs
> 50 g of fresh goats' cheese
> Olive oil

Preparation:

1. Wash the tomatoes, cut them in half and remove the seeds and core of the tomatoes, trying to keep the skin intact. Keep the inside of the tomatoes for the filling.

2. Make a mixture with very finely chopped garlic and parsley, the breadcrumbs, the chopped inside of the tomatoes and a little olive oil and salt.

3. Season the tomatoes before filling them with this mixture.

4. Put the tomatoes on a pre-heated and oiled hot grill plate with the open side up. The grill should not be too hot, so that the tomatoes cook through without burning.

5. When the tomatoes are golden brown on the bottom, turn them carefully with a spatula so they can also brown on top.

6. When the tomatoes are cooked, place them on individual plates, crumble some goats' cheese and a little chopped fresh parsley on top and serve hot.

TOMATES RELLENOS DE HUEVO

Tomatoes Filled with Egg

Ingredients:

> 6 small tomatoes
> 3 eggs, hard-boiled, mashed
> 4 tablespoons of alioli (or mayonnaise seasoned with garlic)
> Salt
> Pepper
> 1 tablespoon of parsley, chopped
> Olive oil

Preparation:

1. Cut the tops off the tomatoes and maybe a slice off the bottom so you can stand them flat.

2. Remove the insides of the tomatoes.

3. Mix the eggs with the alioli, salt, pepper and parsley. If the mixture seems too soft, you may have to add some breadcrumbs.

4. Fill the tomatoes. Sprinkle with some olive oil and black pepper; decorate with a piece of fresh parsley and serve on individual plates.

TOMATES RELLENOS DE PATATA Y CALABACÍN

Tomatoes Filled with Potato and Courgette

Ingredients:

> 1 large potato
> 1 medium courgette
> 3 large tomatoes
> Dill
> Corn flour
> Olive oil
> 1 Onion

Preparation:

1. Clean and cut the potato and courgette into thin slices.

2. Finely chop the onion.

3. Cover the potatoes, courgettes and onions in a pan with olive oil. Place on a medium heat, put the lid on the pan, and leave to cook until the courgette starts to disintegrate and the potato slices are slightly browned. Drain the oil from the mix.

4. Cut the tomatoes in half and scoop out the inside seeds and flesh.

5. Mix a little water and corn flour together until it becomes a slightly thick paste. Mix this with the cooked vegetables. Fill the tomatoes with this mixture.

6. Sprinkle some dill on top of the filling.

7. Place the tomatoes in an oven preheated to 200°C.

8. Bake the tomatoes until the tops are golden brown. Serve the individual tomato halves hot as a tapa on a small plate with a slice of bread.

TOMATITOS RELLENOS DE PÂTÉ DE BERENJENAS
Cherry Tomatoes Filled with Aubergine Pâté

There are many possibilities for making stuffed tomatoes. This is just one example: tomatoes filled with aubergine pâté. You can use any savoury pâté instead, including green or black olive tapenade.

Ingredients:

> 6 cherry tomatoes
> Aubergine pâté (See recipe in the Chapter "Pâtés")
> Sesame seeds
> Sea salt

Preparation:

1. Cut the tomatoes in half and scoop the flesh from the inside. (Keep this for a "tomato on toast" breakfast.)

2. Season the tomatoes and let them stand upside down for a little while.

3. Fill the tomatoes with the aubergine pâté and garnish with toasted sesame seeds.

4. Serve cold with a little bread.

TOMATES RELLENOS DE QUESO CREMA Y HIERBAS

Tomatoes Filled with Cream Cheese and Herbs

Ingredients:

> 6 firm, medium-sized tomatoes
> 100 g of cream cheese
> 1 bunch of fresh herbs or a mixture of dried herbs including oregano, chives, dill, basil, thyme
> Salt to taste
> Pepper to taste
> Olive oil
> 1-2 spring onions

Preparation:

1. Cut the top off the tomatoes, remove the flesh and seeds from inside the tomato and put these aside in a bowl.

2. Add the cream cheese to the tomato pulp with a drop of olive oil. Chop the spring onions and herbs very finely and season with salt and pepper to taste. Add the onion and herbs to the cheese and tomato mix and blend together well.

3. Fill the tomatoes with the mixture, letting it overflow slightly.

4. Add a tablespoon of mayonnaise or alioli to the mixture, if you want a creamier consistency. Serve chilled.

TOMATES VERDES FRITOS

Fried Green Tomatoes

The tomato crop in Spain is prolific. Hence the country has developed a vast array of gastronomic uses for the tomato. Here green tomatoes are used to make a very tasty fried tapa. Wasting food in rural Spain is anathema so this is a typical recipe to use up excess production in an imaginative and delicious way.

Ingredients:

Green tomatoes
Garlic
Parsley
Salt
Breadcrumbs
Egg
Olive oil

Preparation:

1. Wash and dry the tomatoes and cut them into slices of about half a centimetre. Put them into a large colander and add salt.

2. Heat plenty of olive oil in a frying pan.

3. Beat some eggs and add very finely chopped garlic and parsley.

4. Dip the tomato slices in the beaten egg and then coat them in breadcrumbs.

5. Fry the battered tomatoes in small batches so as not to cool the oil too much.

6. When the tomato slices are golden brown, remove them from the oil and place them on kitchen paper to dry.

7. Serve on individual plates, decorated with fresh parsley.

TORTILLA DE TAGARNINAS DE ANDALUCÍA
Omelette of Golden Thistle of Andalucía

Tagarninas, also known as golden thistle (Scolymus hispanicus) is a wild plant that is found in many parts of Spain. It is well known for its pretty yellow flower. The plant has culinary and medicinal uses, with a history going back to ancient Greece, where it was sometimes cultivated.

In Spain, the plant was traditionally harvested during hard times and, given this connotation, the vegetable has only recently come back onto the market again. Although country people have just continued to harvest it as always, many urban chefs are now beginning to experiment with it again. It is harvested by cutting the emerging floret of leaves at ground level. The stalks and leaves are eaten cooked and are sliced into pieces depending on cooking time. If the plant is harvested young then the leaves and stem are quite tender. It is often used in salads, soups and with scrambled eggs.

Ingredients:

>Tagarninas (thistle leaves)
>Olive oil
>Garlic
>Egg
>Salt

Preparation:

1. Wash the thistle leaves thoroughly. When they are cleaned, slice and boil them until they are tender and then drain them.

2. Put some olive oil in a frying pan, brown some garlic and then add the thistles.

3. When these are fried, add the eggs, make the omelette, then serve.

TOMBET MALLORQUÍN
Tombet of Mallorca

Tombet is a traditional vegetable dish from Mallorca and is available at almost every local restaurant on the island. Tombet is the Mallorcan version of the Occitan ratatouille or the Catalan samfaina. Tombet combines layers of sliced potatoes, aubergines and red peppers previously fried in olive oil. The aubergines and red peppers should not be peeled. Courgettes are often added although the original traditional dish does not use them.

The whole is topped with tomatoes fried with garlic and parsley and presented in a way that it looks like a pie without a crust. It can be served hot in the winter or cold in the summer months.

Ingredients:

The tomato sauce:

2 tablespoons of olive oil
2 cloves of garlic, peeled and chopped
Pepper, to taste
Salt, to taste
Half a teaspoon of dried oregano
400 g of chopped tomatoes (pre-cooked)

The vegetable layers:

2 medium-sized potatoes
1 aubergine
1 large courgette (optional)
1 red pepper
1 green pepper
Olive oil
Salt

Preparation:

The tomato sauce:

1. Heat the oil over a low heat. Add the garlic and fry it very gently for about a minute (it shouldn't brown). Add the salt, pepper, oregano and chopped tomatoes.

2. Cover the pan, and leave the tomatoes to simmer for 30 minutes. If the sauce is too dry, add a little more water.

The vegetable layers:

1. Slice the aubergine into 1 cm slices (without peeling it). Lay the slices on a colander, thoroughly sprinkle them with salt and leave to stand for an hour.

2. Meanwhile, peel the potatoes and cut them into 1 cm slices. Heat the olive oil and fry the potato slices over a medium heat until they are slightly browned.

3. While the potatoes are frying, slice the courgette (without peeling it) and the peppers also in 1 cm slices. Put aside.

4. Drain the potatoes and put them on a dish lined with kitchen paper to soak up the excess oil.

5. Fry the courgette until browned. Put them on kitchen paper to drain.

6. Fry the peppers until they are tender. Drain them and put them on kitchen paper.

7. Pat the aubergine slices dry and fry them until tender. Drain them and put them on kitchen paper.

8. When all the vegetables are fried, thoroughly tender and drained, arrange them in small stacks in little individual earthenware oven dishes, spooning some tomato sauce at the base, and then make the vegetable layers: potato, aubergine, courgette and peppers. Add salt after each layer and end each stack of vegetables with some more tomato sauce for topping. Decorate with some parsley.

9. Preheat the oven to 180°C.

10. Place the individual dishes in the pre-heated oven and bake them for 15 minutes.

12. Serve immediately with a little bread.

13. Tombet can also be served at room temperature, especially during the warm summer months.

VERDURAS A LA PLANCHA

Grilled Vegetables

Grilled food is very popular in all Spanish regions but especially in the South, where grilled vegetables are a great favourite. Every home will have a steel grill either to put on the cooker or a separate electrical grill.

This simple recipe for grilled vegetables has many variations and you can simply use whatever vegetables you have to hand. As a tapa, the vegetables are served on a platter and you help yourself to whatever combination you like.

Ingredients:

>1 courgette
>1 aubergine
>8 green asparagus
>1 green pepper
>1 red pepper
>2 tomatoes
>2 carrots
>2 medium-sized potatoes
>2 leaves of basil
>1 sprig of thyme
>Chives cut in strips
>Olive oil
>Vinegar
>Salt and Pepper

Preparation:

1. Heat up the grill iron. Clean all the vegetables and cut the aubergine, carrots and peppers into strips, the potatoes in slices and prepare the asparagus by removing the lower stem. Slice the courgette.

2. Put a little oil on the grill plate, place the vegetables on the plate and lightly season with salt and pepper. Cook on both sides for 6-8 minutes.

3. Peel the tomatoes and cut them into cubes. Grill them until cooked. Put them into a bowl with a little olive oil and some ground pepper. Add the chopped leaves of basil, thyme and the chives. Add a splash of vinegar and mix well. Serve the grilled vegetables together with the tomato vinaigrette.

---oOo---

2.12 Mushroom Tapas

The variety of mushrooms available in Spain represents a great culinary opportunity for the vegetarian cook. Most of Spain has a profusion of wild, edible mushrooms that you can pick yourself (with care) in the autumn and winter. Fresh, cultivated mushrooms of various types are available around the year and there is also a variety of traditional, dried mushroom products which we can use.

Mushrooms are a great favourite in Spanish food and that includes their use in tapas recipes. Their use ranges from a simple fried mushroom tapa with bread to the more complicated stuffed mushrooms with cheese or with various vegetable fillings. Here we give you some traditional, regional examples; there are many more.

CHAMPIÑONES AL AJILLO

Garlic Mushrooms

This is a classic hot tapa recipe that is very easy to make. You can use cultivated mushrooms or your own choice of wild mushrooms; just alter the cooking time to suit.

Ingredients:

> 800 g of large mushrooms
> 6 cloves of garlic
> 2 chilli peppers
> A handful of fresh parsley (chopped)
> Olive oil
> Black pepper
> Salt

Preparation:

1. Cut the ends off the stems and clean the mushrooms thoroughly. Cut the mushrooms up into 4 or 6 largish pieces. Put aside and ensure they are completely dry.

2. Peel and slice the garlic and chop up the fresh parsley. Chop the chilli peppers finely.

3. Sauté the mushrooms without oil for two or three minutes to seal and lightly brown them. Then add some olive oil, the chillies and the garlic. Continue to sauté on a high heat for two or three minutes more, so the mushrooms are cooked, but still juicy.

4. Add a pinch of salt and pepper, and the fresh parsley. Stir again a few times and take off the heat.

5. Serve immediately in small bowls with a slice of bread.

CHAMPIÑONES AL JEREZ - CROCANTE DE PAN

Crispy Bread with Mushrooms in Sherry

Ingredients:

Medium-sized fresh mushrooms
Pine kernels
Olive oil
Butter
Coriander
Sweet sherry (oloroso or similar)
Salt
Pepper
A baguette

Instructions:

1. Clean the mushrooms and cut them into thick slices.

2. Chop the coriander.

3. Fry the mushrooms with the pine kernels in a pan with some olive oil on a low heat. Season with salt and pepper, stir and continue to cook for about 2 minutes.

4. Add enough sherry to just cover the mushrooms and cook over a low heat, uncovered, until the sherry is reduced completely.

5. Let the mushrooms cool and then mix in the chopped coriander.

6. Cut the baguette into thin slices.

7. Spread some butter on each slice and bake them at a medium heat until they are golden brown and crispy.

8. Spread each slice with the mushroom mixture and serve.

CHAMPIÑONES CON ALIOLI

Mushrooms with Garlic Mayonnaise

Ingredients:

> 150 g of mushrooms
> Olive oil
> Salt
> 1 glass of sherry
> Garlic mayonnaise (alioli - see recipe)
> 1 baguette, sliced

Preparation:

1. Clean the mushrooms and slice them thinly.

2. Heat some olive oil in a frying pan. Add the mushrooms, the glass of sherry and some salt to taste to the oil, cover the pan and leave the mushrooms to simmer for about 10 minutes. Drain and set aside.

3. Toast the bread just a little; do not brown.

4. Spread the toast with alioli and then top with the cooked mushrooms.

5. Place the bread and mushrooms under a grill for about 30 seconds or until the alioli starts to bubble.

6. Serve immediately.

CHAMPIÑONES EN VINAGRE

Mushrooms in Vinegar

You can vary this basic mushroom in vinegar recipe according to your taste by adding more or less garlic, chilli pepper(s), basil or other herbs and spices.

Ingredients:

> 250 g of firm mushrooms
> Vinegar (wine or cider, according to your taste)
> Olive oil
> 4 cloves of garlic
> Fresh parsley (chopped)
> 1 chilli pepper (optional)
> Basil (optional)
> Salt to taste

Preparation:

1. Clean the mushrooms well.

2. Cut the mushrooms into slices of about 2-3 mm thick.

3. Layer the slices in a bowl, seasoning each layer.

4. Cover the mushrooms with vinegar. Place a weight on the mushrooms (another bowl or plate) because they tend to float.

5. Leave them to soak for 10 to 20 minutes, depending on how much you like vinegar and on the thickness of the slices. After this time, drain them well.

6. Chop the garlic and parsley and mix with some olive oil. Use this mixture to dress the mushrooms. Cover the bowl and let it marinate in the fridge for at least 4 hours.

7. When marinated, serve the mushrooms on a small plate with a slice of bread or some fried potatoes.

CHAMPIÑONES PICANTES EN SALSA DE VINO
Spicy Mushrooms in Wine Sauce

For this recipe you can use any kind of wild or cultivated mushroom, simply adjust the cooking time to suit. You can make the sauce with a white or a red wine. Adjust the amount of chilli to your own taste.

Ingredients:

> 400 g of mushrooms
> 2 large cloves of garlic
> 150 ml of white (or red) wine
> Half a tablespoon of flour
> 3 tablespoons of olive oil
> Salt
> 2 chilli peppers
> Fresh parsley
> 1 baguette

Preparation:

1. Cut the ends off the stems of the mushrooms. Wash and dry the mushrooms and cut them in half.

2. Finely chop the garlic and the chilli peppers.

3. Fry the garlic in the olive oil. When it starts to brown, add the chilli peppers and the mushrooms. Stir for 1 minute, add the flour and mix well.

4. Pour in the wine and a little water (depending on the thickness of the sauce). Season and leave to cook over a medium heat for about 20 minutes.

5. When the mushrooms are cooked, turn off the heat, sprinkle them with chopped parsley, mix well and serve hot by itself or on slices of baguette.

CHAMPIÑONES RELLENOS DE BATATA

Mushrooms Stuffed with Sweet Potato

This is a simple and delicious recipe for baked mushrooms filled with sweet potato. The recipe is a generic one and has many variations. Indeed, you can fill mushrooms with a huge variety of interesting and delicious ingredients, such as various cheeses, many combinations of vegetables and fruits, topped with béchamel or any other of the popular Spanish savoury sauces.

Ingredients:

> 6 large mushrooms
> 1 medium-sized sweet potato
> 3 cloves of garlic
> 1 small onion
> Salt
> Olive oil
> Rosemary

Preparation:

1. Wash the mushrooms and remove the stems (set aside).

2. Bring some water to the boil in a saucepan. Put the mushrooms into the boiling water for about 5 minutes. Remove and drain.

3. Chop the garlic, the onion, the sweet potato and the mushroom stems into very small pieces.

4. Fry the garlic and onion in some olive oil. When they start to brown, add the sweet potato and the mushroom stems. Add salt and rosemary to taste. Sauté this mixture, stirring occasionally, until tender.

5. Preheat the oven to 200°C.

6. Fill the mushrooms caps with the fried vegetable mix.

7. Put the filled mushrooms into the oven for about 10 minutes, until they start to brown.

8. Serve the filled mushrooms hot. If there is any filling left over, use this to decorate the plate.

CHAMPIÑONES RELLENOS DE PATATA Y HUEVOS MINI

Mushrooms Filled with Quails' Eggs

Ingredients:

12 large mushrooms
12 quails' eggs
2 small potatoes
2 cloves of garlic
6 tablespoons of olive oil
Parsley
Ground pepper
Salt

Preparation:

1. Wash and boil the potatoes in salted water for about 20-25 minutes. Let them cool slightly, then peel and mash them. Mix in 1 tablespoon of olive oil and some salt and pepper.

2. Take the stems off the mushrooms and wash and dry the mushrooms. Salt them. Preheat the oven to 200°C.

3. Chop the garlic very finely and sauté it in a pan for a few minutes with a tablespoon of olive oil.

4. Mix the garlic with the potato and fill the mushrooms with the mixture.

5. Bake the mushrooms for 10 minutes at 200°C.

6. Meanwhile, heat the remaining olive oil in a frying pan and fry the quails' eggs carefully, using a small mold.

7. Arrange one fried egg on each mushroom, season and garnish with a little chopped parsley.

CHAMPIÑONES RELLENOS DE TORTA DEL CASAR
Mushrooms Filled with Cheese of Extremadura

Torta del Casar (D.O.) is a creamy cheese made from sheep milk in the Extremadura region of Spain. It is named after Casar de Cáceres, its city of origin. The combination of mushrooms and the creamy and strong sheep cheese makes a delicious tapa. If you cannot find Torta del Casar easily, you can substitute another young sheep cheese as the base.

Ingredients:

> 300 g of large mushrooms
> Torta del Casar
> 2 tomatoes
> Olive oil
> Grated mature sheep cheese

Preparation:

1. Chop the tomatoes into small cubes. Fry them in olive oil for 3 to 4 minutes. Set aside.

2. Remove the mushroom stalks and put them aside for another dish. Wash the mushroom caps very well and allow them to dry thoroughly.

3. Place the caps upside down and spoon some torta del Casar cheese at the bottom of each mushroom cap. Cover with the cooked tomato cubes.

4. Put the mushrooms in a preheated oven to bake at 170°C for 15 minutes.

5. After that time, take the mushrooms out of the oven, sprinkle some grated cheese on them and put them back into the oven until they are gratinated.

6. Place each mushroom on a small plate and serve hot (with a slice of bread, if required).

CHAMPIÑONES CON SALSA DE CERVEZA

Mushrooms with Beer Sauce

You can use any type of beer for this recipe, but a lager is suggested rather than a heavier beer.

Ingredients:

600 g of mushrooms
2 shallots
3 cloves of garlic
300 ml of beer
A few sprigs of fresh thyme
Rosemary (optional - to your taste)
60 ml of water
1 teaspoon of cornstarch
A small handful of toasted pine kernels (optional)
Black pepper
1 chilli pepper
Salt
Olive oil

Preparation:

1. Cut the ends off the mushrooms' stems. Thoroughly wash and subsequently dry the mushrooms. Cut them into quarters.

2. Peel the shallots and garlic and chop them up. Fry the shallots and garlic in olive oil until they start to brown and then add the mushrooms (and -optionally- the pine nuts).

3. Increase the heat, add salt and pepper to taste and more olive oil if needed. Fry the mixture for a couple of minutes, stirring occasionally, and then add the thyme, (rosemary), chilli and beer.

4. When the mixture starts to boil again, lower the heat to medium and let the mix simmer for about 20 minutes or until the mushrooms are tender.

5. Add the cornstarch dissolved in a little water and cook for a few more minutes, until the sauce thickens. Taste to see if it has enough salt and pepper and add more as required. Serve the hot mushrooms in small dishes with a piece of bread.

CREMA DE SETAS EN TOSTADA

Cream of Mushrooms on Toast

Ingredients

450-500 g of fresh mushrooms
1 shallot
2 cloves of garlic
3 sprigs of thyme (and/or rosemary and sage, to taste)
Black pepper
Olive oil
Salt
6-8 tablespoons of evaporated milk
Mature sheep cheese (grated)
4 large slices of crusty bread

Preparation:

1. Peel the shallot, cut it in half and then chop very finely. Peel the garlic and cut it into slices.

2. Fry the shallot in olive oil on a low heat. When it begins to soften, add half of the garlic, turn up the heat and cook until browning. Now add the mushrooms and season with salt, freshly ground black pepper and thyme.

3. Cook the mushrooms until the liquid has evaporated. Add the remaining garlic and sauté until browned.

3. Add the evaporated milk, varying the amount you use according to how creamy you wish the mushrooms to be. Mix well and simmer for one or two minutes before removing the pan from the heat.

4. Toast or grill the bread, adding a little olive oil as desired.

5. Serve the creamed mushrooms hot on the slices of toast with some grated sheep cheese on each. Decorate with fresh thyme.

MORRETE DE SETAS

Mushroom Casserole

This is a traditional mushroom casserole of central Andalucía, made with wild or cultivated mushrooms. We suggest oyster mushrooms.

Ingredients:

> 1 kg of oyster mushrooms
> 3 cloves of garlic
> 1 tablespoon of sweet paprika powder
> 1 slice of hard (dry) cateto bread
> Olive oil
> Vinegar
> Salt

Preparation:

1. Fry the cloves of garlic (unpeeled) in a frying pan with a little olive oil until they are golden.

2. Peel the garlic and put them in a mortar with salt, a tablespoon of olive oil, paprika powder, the bread and a splash of vinegar. Grind the mixture well until you get a smooth paste.

3. Sauté the chopped mushrooms in the same oil. When they are tender, add the majado (paste) and a little water.

4. Stir gently and simmer for about 10 minutes.

5. Serve hot on small plates with a small piece of crusty bread.

PIQUILLOS DE CHAMPIÑONES

Mushroom Filled Peppers

Ingredients:

1 jar of piquillo peppers
200 g of mushrooms
4 tablespoons of rolled oats
1 small onion
4 medium-sized carrots
4 cloves of garlic
250 ml of water
8 tablespoons of olive oil
1 splash of white wine
Salt
Black pepper
Nutmeg

Preparation:

1. Cover the oats with water.

2. Clean and slice the mushrooms. Fry the mushrooms in olive oil. When they release their juices, add the crushed garlic, the parsley and the drained oats. Season to taste. Stir well and then remove the pan from the heat.

3. Fill the piquillo peppers with the mixture and place them in casserole dishes.

4. Prepare the carrot sauce in a saucepan by first frying the finely chopped onion in olive oil. When the onions are soft, add the sliced carrots. Stir the mixture well and add the wine. When the wine has evaporated, add 250 ml of water.

5. Boil the sauce until the carrots are tender (about 20 minutes). Season the sauce.

6. Finally, put the mixture in a blender and blend until obtaining a fine-textured sauce. Add more hot water until the sauce has a creamy and smooth consistency.

7. Serve the stuffed peppers hot, with a little of the carrot sauce.

TOSTA DE SETAS CON HUEVO

Mushroom and Hardboiled Egg

Ingredients:

2 eggs
Olive oil
2 large slices of rustic bread
250 g of mixed wild mushrooms
2 cloves of garlic, minced
1 small shallot, finely chopped
1 teaspoon of chopped thyme
1 teaspoon of lemon juice
Salt
Freshly ground black pepper

Preparation:

1. Hard-boil the eggs and then put them aside for 10 minutes. When cool, peel the eggs and break them up into small pieces with a fork.

2. Coat the slices of bread with olive oil. Grill or toast until lightly browned. Set aside.

3. Meanwhile, fry the mushrooms in olive oil, stirring and tossing occasionally, until well browned on all sides (about 5 minutes). Add the garlic, shallot, and thyme and cook, stirring constantly for a few seconds. Add lemon juice and toss to coat.

4. Take the pan off the heat; season the mix with salt and pepper.

5. Serve the mushrooms in small bowls on the toast, accompanied by a sprinkling of hardboiled egg and a few drops of olive oil.

---o0o---

2.13 Tortillas

The tortilla is to Spain what quiche or crêpe is to France. The world of tortillas is virtually infinite. The culinary history of the tortilla goes back a very long time and crosses continents. The Romans called them "ovorum cake", in Mexico they have made them for thousands of years as have the Native American tribes in the U.S.

The simplest tortilla is a fried, whisked egg (omelette), but up from that they can reach a level of extraordinary sophistication. They can be sweet or savoury, and the range of ingredients includes all vegetables and many fruits. They can be made with many kinds of flour or with none. They may be thin, soft, brittle, thick, dry or oily. They can be fried or baked and can even be made without eggs.

A particular type of tortilla is very popular in Spain, and this tortilla is normally made with eggs. In all of Spain, pieces of tortilla are often served as a tapa, alone or with a slice of bread and accompanied, for example, with a sauce such as alioli (garlic mayonnaise), red pepper sauce or "sofrito" (fried tomato sauce).

Here we present a selection of popular Spanish tortilla recipes.

TORTILLA DE PATATAS

Spanish Omelette

There are an almost infinite number of tortilla recipes. Almost anything can go into a tortilla. Tortillas are served alone or with a vast array of accompanying sauces. This is the basic traditional potato and onion version that you can find throughout Spain.

Ingredients:

> 6-7 medium-sized potatoes, peeled
> 1 onion
> 5-6 large eggs
> 500 ml of olive oil for frying
> Salt (to taste)

Preparation:

1. Cut the peeled potatoes into pieces of approximately half a centimetre.

2. Peel and chop the onion into small pieces. Put potatoes and onions into a bowl and mix them together. Add salt to taste.

3. Pour the olive oil into a large, heavy, non-stick frying pan and heat it on medium heat. Put in the potatoes and onions to fry. The oil should just cover the potatoes. Keep stirring and do not allow the potatoes to burn. As soon as the potatoes are tender, remove the pan from the heat. Take out the potatoes and onions with a slotted spoon, allowing the oil to drain off. Put aside.

4. Crack the eggs into a large mixing bowl and whisk them together. Stir in the potato and onion mix.

5. Pour 1-2 tablespoons of olive oil into a non-stick frying pan and heat to medium.

6. Still stirring, pour the mix into the pan and spread it out evenly. Allow the egg to cook around the edges. Be careful not to get the pan too hot because the tortilla will burn.

7. Lift up one side of the omelette to check if the egg is beginning to brown. The inside of the mixture should not be completely cooked and the egg will still be a bit soft.

When the mixture has browned on the bottom, flip the omelette (using a plate) and cook the other side.

8. Use a spatula to shape the sides of the omelette. When cooked through and light brown take the pan off the heat and leave the omelette to stand for 2 minutes.

9. Slide the omelette onto a plate to serve, cut into 6-8 pieces like a pie.

10. Serve as a tapa alone or with a slice of bread, or together with some sofrito (a fried tomato sauce made with tomatoes, onions, garlic, green peppers and olive oil sautéed in a frying pan), some alioli or simply with some slices of fresh tomato.

11. In Rioja, a popular variant of this tapa is served with a topping of local spicy red peppers called "alegrias".

TORTILLA DE BERENJENAS

Aubergine Tortilla

Ingredients:

> 500 g of aubergine
> 1 large onion
> Olive oil
> 5 eggs
> Coarse salt

Preparation:

1. Clean the aubergine and cut it into slices, discarding the stem. Coat the slices lightly with salt and allow to stand for about 10 minutes. Dry the aubergine.

2. Peel the onion, cut it into rings and fry these in olive oil. Add the dried slices of aubergine and fry until golden brown. Remove and drain.

3. Beat the eggs, add the aubergine and onion and mix all together. Season the mixture and pour it into a frying pan with a little hot olive oil. Fry the omelette slowly on a moderate heat.

4. Let it cook for about 5 minutes, then turn the tortilla and let it brown on the other side.

5. When fully browned, cut the tortillas into triangles and serve hot or cold.

TORTILLA DE CALABACÍN

Courgette Tortilla

Ingredients:

> 6 eggs
> 200 ml olive oil
> Mayonnaise
> 1 kg of unpeeled courgettes
> 2 chopped onions
> Salt
> Country bread (cateto or similar)

Preparation:

1. Slowly fry the onions, seasoned with salt, in about 100 ml of olive oil.

2. Wash the courgettes and, without peeling them, cut them into thin slices. Fry those together with the onions until the onions become translucent. Don't fry too much or the courgettes will loose their flavour.

3. When they are ready, remove the courgettes and onions from the pan and put them into a colander to drain off the oil.

4. Beat the eggs in a bowl and season them. Then stir in the courgettes and onions and mix well.

5. Heat another 100 ml of olive oil in a non-stick frying pan. Add the tortilla mixture. Reduce the heat to allow the tortilla to slowly cook and solidify.

6. Use a pan lid or a plate to turn the omelette to cook it on the other side.

7. Serve pieces of the tortilla on a slice of country bread (cateto or similar) spread with mayonnaise.

TORTILLA DE ESPÁRRAGOS TRIGUEROS

Green Asparagus Tortilla

Ingredients:

> 4 spears of asparagus
> 3 tablespoons of olive oil
> 3 tablespoons of cream
> 4 eggs
> Freshly ground white pepper
> Salt

Preparation:

1. Wash the asparagus and chop them into small pieces. Set aside the asparagus tips, and boil the bottom halves of the stems in salty water for 10 minutes. Chill immediately in iced water.

2. Heat 2 tablespoons of olive oil in a pan and fry all the asparagus pieces for about 3 minutes. Remove and put aside.

3. Whisk the eggs with the cream in a bowl.

4. Heat the remaining oil in the pan and pour in the egg mixture. Let the mix solidify slightly and arrange the asparagus on top.

5. Shake the pan to ensure that the asparagus are well-covered with the egg mixture.

6. Fry the tortilla on both sides, season with salt and pepper and serve hot.

TORTILLA DE ESPINACAS

Spinach Tortilla

Ingredients:

> 300 g of spinach leaves (frozen)
> 1 clove of garlic
> Freshly ground white pepper
> Salt
> Freshly grated nutmeg
> 4 tablespoons of olive oil
> 4 eggs
> 3 tablespoons of cream

Preparation:

1. Let the spinach leaves slowly thaw and drain well.

2. Crush the garlic and mix it with a little oil. Heat 1 tablespoon of oil in a pan and stir-fry the spinach for 5 minutes.

3. Season the spinach with garlic, pepper, salt and nutmeg.

4. Whisk the eggs together with the cream.

5. Heat the remaining oil in a pan, pour in the egg mixture and cover this immediately with the spinach. Let it cook on a medium heat for about 8 minutes.

6. A variant of this recipe uses some grated goats' cheese sprinkled on the finished tortilla and melted under a grill.

7. Serve a slice of the hot tortilla alone or with a small slice of bread.

TORTILLA DE HIERBAS AROMÁTICAS

Tortilla with Fresh Herbs

Ingredients:

> 1 teaspoon of fresh tarragon, finely chopped
> 1 teaspoon of fresh oregano leaves, chopped
> 1 teaspoon of fresh thyme leaves
> 1 teaspoon of fresh parsley, chopped
> 4 eggs
> 3 tablespoons of cream
> Freshly ground white pepper
> Salt
> Nutmeg
> 3 tablespoons of olive oil
> 2 tablespoons of grated Manchego cheese

Preparation:

1. Mix the fresh herbs with the eggs and the cream in a bowl. Season the mixture with pepper, salt and freshly grated nutmeg.

2. Heat the olive oil in a frying pan.

3. Make 2 thin tortillas with the egg mixture.

4. When ready, take them out of the pan and roll them up.

5. Place them in an oven-proof dish and sprinkle both with the grated cheese.

6. Briefly bake under a grill until the cheese melts and browns slightly.

7. Serve hot.

TORTILLA DE PAN RALLADO

Breadcrumb Tortilla

Here is one recipe that shows once again the ingenuity and talent of the cooks of Andalucía, who use the simplest ingredients they have on hand, and are able to prepare delicious dishes from almost nothing.

Ingredients:

> 8 eggs
> 1 clove of garlic
> 50 g of breadcrumbs
> Parsley
> Salt

Preparation:

1. Beat the egg whites together first and then add the egg yolks. Add garlic, very finely chopped parsley, and salt.

2. Stir in the breadcrumbs and mix well until the batter has the right consistency.

3. Bake the tortilla over a low heat, to make sure that it is cooked inside. Shape into a circular shaped "cake".

TORTILLA PIMIENTOS

Pepper Tortilla

Ingredients:

> 1 red pepper
> 1 green pepper
> 2 beef tomatoes
> 5 spring onions
> 5 cloves of garlic
> 4 tablespoons olive oil
> Freshly ground black pepper
> Salt
> 4 chopped olives
> 4 eggs

Preparation:

1. Wash the peppers, cut them in half and remove the seeds. Put them on a baking tray and bake them in a pre-heated oven at 250°C for about 20 minutes.

2. Remove the tray from the oven; cover the peppers with a damp cloth and leave to cool. Peel the peppers and cut them into thin strips.

3. Skin the tomatoes, de-seed them and chop them into small pieces. Wash the spring onions and cut them into small rings. Peel and crush the garlic.

4. Heat half the olive oil in a frying pan. Lightly fry the onions and garlic. Add the peppers and tomatoes. Season with salt, pepper and olives, and simmer until all liquid is absorbed. Put the vegetable mix in a bowl and leave aside.

5. Pour the rest of the oil into the same frying pan and heat it up. Whisk the eggs, season with salt and pepper, and pour into the pan. Let them solidify on a low heat for 3-4 minutes.

6. Spread the vegetable mixture over the eggs in the pan, cover and cook for a further 8-10 minutes.

7. Serve.

TORTILLA DE QUESO RONCAL AL HORNO
Oven-baked Roncal Cheese Tortilla

Roncal cheese comes from the rich sheep milk of the famous Lacha and Aragonesa breeds of sheep. Depending on the season, these herds graze in the high Pyrenees or in the Bardenas area of Navarra. Roncal, made and matured in one of seven villages in the Valle de Roncal, has a strong flavour and a firm texture and is similar to Manchego. Roncal is a D.O. protected product.

For those wanting to reduce the oil content of their tortillas: it is possible to bake them in the oven instead of frying them. This recipe minimises the use of oil and, if you want to reduce the fat content further, you can also reduce the amount of cheese.

Ingredients:

> 1 red pepper
> 150 g of grated cheese (Roncal or similar)
> 5 eggs
> Salt, to taste
> Pepper, to taste
> 2 garlic cloves
> 3 boiled potatoes
> 4 spring onions
> Olive oil for frying
> 1 green pepper
> 75 g of sour cream
> 2 tablespoons of chives

Preparation:

1. Line a shallow rectangular baking dish with aluminium foil and rub on some oil. Preheat the oven to 180°C.

2. Peel and crush the garlic.

3. Clean and chop the chives.

4. Wash the peppers, cut them in half, remove the seeds and stem. Cut into cubes.

5. Heat a little oil in a frying pan, fry the onion and then add the crushed garlic.

6. Add the peppers and stir-fry all for about 8 minutes.

7. Let the mix cool.

8. Cut the potatoes into small cubes and mix them with the sautéed vegetables.

9. Beat the eggs and add the cream, grated cheese, chives and the vegetables from the pan. Mix everything together well and add salt and pepper to taste.

10. Pour the mixture into the pre-prepared mould and smooth the surface.

11. Bake the tortilla in the middle of the oven for about 35 minutes.

12. Remove the omelette from the oven, cut it into cubes or slices and serve hot as a tapa.

2.14 Stews and Fricassees

In the more temperate parts of Spain and during the winter in many parts of the interior of the peninsula, a tapa may well consist of a hearty, warming stew. Spain is a very mountainous country and much of the centre and north of the country faces very cold winters, often with bitter mountain winds. During the autumn and winter, a welcome evening respite from a day harvesting olives or working on the land may be a small bowl of hot stew with bread and a glass of wine. This rural tradition has spread to the cities and there are many such tapas available everywhere.

ALIÑO DE ESPÁRRAGOS DE GRANADA
Asparagus Stew of Granada

This recipe comes from the West of the province of Granada which is famous for its production of green asparagus.

Ingredients:

> 400 g of green asparagus
> 3 cloves of garlic
> Coarse breadcrumbs
> Vinegar (to taste)
> Salt (to taste)
> A pinch of saffron

Preparation:

1. Boil the asparagus with a little salt. Drain them and set them aside when they are about half cooked (10-12 minutes).

2. Fry the chopped garlic in a separate pan and set aside. Make a majado paste in a mortar with the breadcrumbs and a little oil.

3. Add the asparagus together with the majado to the frying pan with the garlic, and add a dash of vinegar, a pinch of salt, a pinch of saffron and a little water. (Sometimes a beaten egg is also added to the mixture at this point).

4. Cook the mixture for about 5 minutes and serve in small bowls with a slice of bread.

CAZUELA DE HABAS (II)

Broad Bean Casserole(II)

This is a traditional late winter casserole dish from the cool mountainous regions of Andalucía. Broad beans grow exceptionally well in the south of Spain and in April they are abundant. To maintain a year-round supply, the beans are often dried for storage. This dish can be made with either dried or fresh beans.

Ingredients:

> 2 kg of broad beans
> 0.5 kg of artichokes
> Some lettuce leaves
> 1 large tomato
> 1 pepper
> 1 onion
> 100 g of almonds
> 1 bay leaf
> Black pepper
> Olive oil
> Food colouring (e.g. saffron)
> Salt
> Garlic

Preparation:

1. Fry the almonds in the olive oil, and set them aside.

2. Prepare a sofrito: In the same oil used for the almonds, fry the tomato (peeled), the finely chopped pepper and onion, and add salt, pepper and garlic to your own taste.

3. When the sofrito is cooked, add the almonds, blend it all together and set aside.

4. Put the beans, artichokes and lettuce in a bowl of water with a few drops of lemon juice. Drain and put them in a saucepan with water. Add the sofrito (already prepared), together with the food colouring and the bay leaf.

5. Cook over a medium heat for half an hour.

6. Serve it hot in small bowls.

CHANFAINA VIUDA DE MÁLAGA

Widows' Stew - Vegetable Stew of Málaga

Chanfaina is the local name for a cod stew in Málaga province, but this version of the stew is made without cod or any meat substitute, just vegetables - hence the name "Widows' Stew". The widows' stew is a typical recipe for Easter, but it is often made as a tapa using whatever vegetables are to hand.

Ingredients:

> 0.25 kg of potato
> 0.25 kg of pumpkin
> 0.25 kg of onion
> 0.25 kg of aubergines or courgettes
> 0.25 kg of oyster mushrooms
> 4 or 5 cloves of garlic
> 150 g almonds
> 1 teaspoon of oregano
> 2 slices of cateto bread (yesterday's), crumbled
> 1 tablespoon of vinegar (to taste)
> Saffron
> Olive oil
> Salt (to taste)

Preparation:

1. Grind up the peeled almonds, salt, oregano, breadcrumbs, vinegar, saffron and the garlic in a mortar, making them into a smooth paste (majado). Stir in a glass of water to thin the paste. Put it aside.

2. Wash, peel and dice the potatoes, chop up the pumpkin and onion, cut the aubergines and mushrooms into strips and stir-fry all together until tender but not browned.

3. Drain the oil from the vegetables. Add the majado paste and stir gently (don't purée it). Cover and simmer for a few minutes, gently shaking the pan.

4. Serve hot with a slice of bread.

GUISO ALBORONÍA

Stew Alboronía (Vegetable Stew)

The name of this dish originates from the Arabic al-buraniyya. This word derived from the name of the woman Buran who was the wife of caliph al Ma'mun. The Arabic term buraniyya means stew. The dish and its name are a further illustration of the profound influence the Arab culinary habits exerted on the Christian cuisine in Andalucía. The recipe presented here is just one of many variations. In Catalán it is called "xanfaina", and in Aragón it is called "fritada". It makes an excellent, simple, but tasty tapa.

Ingredients:

> 4 aubergines
> 2 peppers
> 4 tomatoes
> 2 onions,
> Half a pumpkin
> Paprika powder
> Vinegar
> Olive oil
> Salt

Preparation:

1. Wash the aubergines, clean and peel the pumpkin and cut both into medium-sized pieces.

2. Wash the peppers and remove the seeds. Cut the peppers into strips.

3. Wash, skin and de-seed the tomatoes and chop them very finely.

4. Fry the peppers and onions in oil. When they are browned, add the tomatoes. Sauté for a moment, then add the aubergines and pumpkin. Season with salt and paprika powder whilst stirring, and then add vinegar to taste.

5. Cover the pan, and leave the vegetables to simmer gently until everything is tender but still firm.

6. Serve hot in small bowls.

PEPITORIA CON PATATAS

Potato and Vegetable Fricassee

A pepitoria is traditionally a method of cooking fowl and is thought to originate in Arab culinary tradition. In this version of the fricassee, the meat has been replaced by potatoes. This substitution of meat for vegetables was common during religious feast days when the eating of meat was not permitted.

Ingredients:

> 700 g of potatoes
> Flour to coat the potatoes
> 2 eggs
> Olive oil
> Half an onion
> 2 cloves of garlic
> Salt
> 1 teaspoon of flour
> 150 ml of white wine
> 1 bay leaf
> Black pepper
> Parsley
> Half a teaspoon of yellow food colouring

Preparation:

1. Cut the potatoes into thick slices of about two centimetres. Coat them in flour with some egg. Fry them in plenty of hot oil.

2. When the potatoes are golden brown take them off the heat and put aside.

3. Make a sofrito by finely chopping and frying the onions in olive oil with a pinch of salt. Before the onions start to brown, crush the garlic with parsley and a pinch of salt and add to the onions but don't let the mix brown. Add a teaspoon of flour to thicken the sauce and stir a few times so that the flour is just cooked, but not browning.

4. Now add the potatoes to the pan, placing them flat in the bottom of the pan. Add the white wine, bay leaf, pepper and the food colouring.

5. When it has reduced a little, cover with water, but only to the top of the potatoes.

6. Simmer until the potatoes are tender. If need be, add more water if the mix becomes dry before the potatoes are tender.

7. Serve the potatoes hot with a spoonful of sauce in small individual bowls. You can also prepare this tapa in advance and just grill each dish for a few minutes before serving the tapas hot.

PISTO MANCHEGO
Pisto of La Mancha

Pisto of La Mancha is a traditional regional dish which has now spread throughout Spain. It is often called "Moje" in La Mancha. It is a kind of peasant vegetable stew based on tomatoes but with a fairly variable list of vegetable ingredients depending on the season and what vegetables were to hand. This particular recipe comes from Albacete. Traditionally, it was placed in the centre of the table and dipped into with bread by all the diners until it was all gone.

Ingredients:

>2 medium-sized courgettes
>3 green peppers
>1 red pepper
>1 kg of ripe tomatoes
>1 onion
>Olive oil
>Salt

Preparation:

1. Clean the vegetables and remove the pepper seeds. Cut the peppers into small pieces. Cut the courgettes into cubes. Skin the tomatoes if you wish.

2. Sauté the onions on a low heat and then add the peppers with some salt. Keep turning to prevent burning. Add the cubes of courgette to the pan when the onion and peppers are about half cooked.

3. When we see that the vegetables are almost cooked, add the tomatoes.

4. Fry all the vegetables together and for a few minutes, stirring occasionally.

5. When completely cooked, the dish can be served hot or cold as a tapa, alone or with bread or toast.

POTAJE CALEÑO DE ANDALUCÍA
Vegetable Stew of Andalucía

This soup-stew is a traditional dish of Eastern Andalucía It is very simple to make, with very little fat and is a warming winter tapa.

Ingredients:

> 400 g of chickpeas
> 80 g of rice
> 2 ripe tomatoes
> 1 pepper
> 2 onions
> 1 bay leaf
> 1 head of garlic
> 2 cloves of garlic
> Black peppercorns (to taste)
> Half a teaspoon of paprika powder
> Saffron
> Olive oil
> Salt (to taste)

Preparation:

1. Soak the chickpeas in water overnight.

2. Put the head of garlic directly on the heat to roast, without breaking it up. Put aside.

3. Bring a pan of water to the boil. Add the chickpeas, the roasted head of garlic, bay leaf, pepper, one onion (peeled and coarsely chopped), and a peeled and chopped tomato. Season and let this simmer until the chickpeas are tender. In a pressure cooker this takes about 20 minutes. If cooked in a normal saucepan, make sure that the dish doesn't stop boiling when water is added. (Use boiling water.)

4. While the chickpeas are cooking, prepare the sofrito: Chop an onion and pepper finely and fry them in olive oil. When the onion is starting to cook, add the other peeled and finely chopped tomato and finally, away from the heat, add the paprika powder. Stir well.

5. Make a majaíllo: Grind the remaining two cloves of garlic and a little salt in a mortar, together with pepper and saffron. Put aside.

6. When the chickpeas are tender, add the sofrito and majaíllo to the pan, together with the rice. Leave the dish to simmer for another 20 minutes to cook the rice.

7. Serve in small bowls with a slice of bread.

POTAJE DE HABAS SECAS

Broad Bean Stew

Ingredients:

      Half a kilo of dried broad beans
      1 medium-sized onion
      2 potatoes
      1 head of garlic (roasted)
      Bay leaf
      Olive oil
      Salt
      Pepper
      80 g of rice

Preparation:

1. Soak the broad beans in water overnight.

2. Peel, cut and par-boil the potatoes. Drain and put aside.

3. Boil the beans in a saucepan with water. Optionally, you can add a handful of white kidney beans

4. Make a sofrito by frying the onions, garlic, pepper, bay leaf and salt. Add to the broad beans.

5. Just before the beans are fully cooked, add a handful of rice and the par-boiled potatoes and continue the cooking until the rice is tender.

6. Serve hot in small bowls.

---oOo---

2.15 Empanadas and Pies

Empanadas are pies and pasties made with various fillings. They originated in the Middle East around the 10th Century CE, made their way to India and Pakistan and arrived in Spain during the Moorish period. The so-called "samosa" is still popular across the Middle East, Asia and North Africa to this day, has a wide range of fillings and many local names and variants.

The origin of the empanada was the need to preserve food by baking (or frying) it into a strong pastry "envelope". This process had the dual result of sterilising the food and giving it several days of extra life. This was particularly important in the hot climates of the Arab countries, including Spain, where travellers and farm workers were often obliged to eat on the road or out in the field.

There are examples of empanadas in many countries: from the Far East, Middle East through to Latin-America, brought there by the Spanish and Portuguese "conquistadores". Some even claim that dishes such as apple strudel originated in Spain's Arab past as a way of preserving apples and raisins in a pastry envelope and brought to Germany and Austria during Spain's control of the Habsburg Empire.

Even within Spain there is a huge range of empanadas. The shape also varies considerably: from a semi-circular pasty shape to round pie shapes to small triangular folded pastry "envelopes", all generally known as empanadillas, up to full- sized savoury pies, served in slices called empanadas.

Empanadillas and empanadas make excellent tapas because they are either small or easy to cut into small portions. They are quite easy to make. They are served either alone or with a variety of accompanying sauces.

There are a number of new variations on the basic empanada which use modern baking techniques to bring new possibilities to this old dish. These modernisations include making open tarts with pre-made pastry of various kinds and focussing on the fillings, and the use of puff pastry, for example. Ultimately though, they are all forms of empanada.

EMPANADA DE ESPINACAS CON CHAMPIÑONES

Mushroom, Goats' Cheese and Spinach Empanada

Ingredients:

For the filling:

> 150 g of onion
> 2 cloves of garlic
> 300 g of fresh spinach
> 200 g of mushrooms
> 150 g of goats' cheese
> 150 ml of cream
> 1 teaspoon of fine cornmeal
> Raisins and pine kernels (optional)

For the dough:

> 250 g of flour
> 6 g of fresh yeast
> 125 ml of water
> 3 tablespoons of olive oil
> 1 teaspoon of salt
> 1 teaspoon of sugar

Preparation:

1. The dough is similar to that used for pizzas. Put all the dough ingredients in a bowl and mix them together well.

2. When thoroughly mixed, place the dough on a lightly floured surface and knead for about 10 minutes until the dough becomes smooth and elastic. Let it rest in a warm place in a covered, lightly greased bowl until it has doubled in volume. This will take about an hour.

3. Clean and slice the mushrooms. Wash the spinach and remove the stems, drain and chop it up a little.

4. Fry the onion in a pan with some olive oil until tender but not browned. Add the mushrooms with the chopped garlic and a little salt. Fry until done and the moisture released from the mushrooms has evaporated. Then stir in the spinach and allow it to lose its volume and surplus moisture.

5. Add the goats' cheese, stirring well to incorporate.

6. Sprinkle in the corn flour, sauté and then add in the cream. Season and cook everything for 5-10 minutes, until all is well mixed and slightly thickened. Allow the mix to cool.

7. Re-fold the dough on a lightly floured surface. Divide into 2 unequal parts (one part for the pie base and one part for the pie top).

8. Roll out the larger portion to the desired size and shape it into the pie mold.

9. Pour the filling of spinach, cheese and mushrooms onto the pastry base without reaching the edges. Cover this with the remaining piece of rolled dough.

10. Seal the edges with a fork and put the pie in a preheated oven at 200°C for 25-30 minutes.

11. Remove the pie from the oven when it is golden brown and let it cool on a rack.

12. Serve small portions of the pie, hot or cold.

EMPANADA DE ESPINACAS Y REQUESÓN

Empanada with Spinach and Cottage Cheese

This is a pie made with spinach and a type of cottage cheese found in Spain called "requesón". You can also use ricotta. It uses a puff pastry casing.

Ingredients:

> A slice of puff pastry dough
> 200 g of requesón or ricotta cheese (or cottage cheese)
> 200 g of spinach

Preparation:

1. Blanch the spinach, drain it very well and chop it finely.

2. Mix the cheese with the spinach, once it has cooled.

3. Cover a baking tray with greaseproof paper and place a thin layer of puff pastry on top. Spread the spinach - cheese mix on the pastry, place another sheet of puff pastry on top of the filing and seal it very well.

4. Place the pie in a pre-heated oven and bake it for around 30 minutes at 175°C.

5. Take the pie out of the oven, cut it into small slices and serve these on small plates.

EMPANADILLA DE VERDURAS

Vegetable Empanadilla

Ingredients:

For the pastry:

      Pastry for 12 small empanadas (circular 10-15 cm in diameter)
      Flour
      Olive oil

For the filling:

      1 chopped onion
      2 cloves of garlic, finely chopped
      Salt to taste
      Pepper to taste
      Oregano to taste
      50 ml of olive oil
      300 ml of florets of broccoli, cooked
      300 ml of florets of cauliflower, cooked
      300 ml of diced carrots, cooked
      2 tablespoons of flour
      380 ml of hot milk

Preparation:

1. Sauté the onion and garlic with a pinch of salt in olive oil. Add the broccoli, cauliflower and carrots. Mix well and sprinkle with flour.

2. Gradually add the hot milk, stirring gently until the filling becomes creamy. Season the mix with salt, pepper and oregano. Allow it to cool.

3. Roll out the pastry and cut out small circular shapes. Place a spoonful of filling mixture in the centre of each circle. Fold them over and brush the edges with water, close them and seal them with a fork.

4. Arrange the empanadas on a floured oven tray and sprinkle them with olive oil.

5. Bake them in a pre-heated oven at about 200°C until golden brown (about 15 minutes).

6. Remove the empanadas from the oven and serve them immediately on individual plates with a sauce of your choice.

PANIZAS GADITANAS DE GARBANZOS
Chickpea Flour Pancakes

The paniza is a kind of pancake made from chickpea flour. Chickpea flour has been used for centuries in India, throughout the Levant, and often in the Mediterranean cuisine, too. In Spanish cuisine the flour is an important ingredient for the famous "tortillitas", which are a type of fritter from Cádiz: vegetables fried in a chickpea batter. Here we have a simplified chickpea batter pancake tapa.

Ingredients:

> 280 ml of chickpea flour
> 500 ml of water
> Salt
> Pepper
> Olive oil for frying

Preparation:

1. Mix all ingredients and let the mix stand for a couple of hours.

2. Boil the mixture in a saucepan, stirring constantly for about 5 minutes, until it forms a thick creamy batter. Remove from the heat.

3. Put the mixture in a bowl and allow to stand until it solidifies. This is best done the day before the batter is needed, or put it in the fridge for a few hours.

4. Cut the dough into thick slices and fry these in plenty of olive oil until golden brown.

5. Serve the panizas on a small plate with a little salad.

TARTALETAS DE ALCACHOFA, QUESO Y CEBOLLINO
Artichoke, Cheese and Onion Tarts

Ingredients:

Puff pastry or short crust pastry
3 eggs
200 ml of light cream (around 18% fat)
140 g of natural yogurt
A pinch of salt
A pinch of black pepper
Half a teaspoon of tarragon
Half a teaspoon of onion powder
Goats' cheese ("Rulo de Queso de Cabra")
Artichoke hearts (frozen or from a jar)
Fresh chives

Preparation:

1. Prepare the topping by mixing the eggs, the cream and yogurt together with a pinch of salt and pepper, the tarragon and the onion powder in a blender. Put aside.

2. Roll out the pastry with a rolling pin and cut circles slightly larger than the base of the tarts, using the tart molds themselves as a guide.

3. Grease the molds with oil or butter. Place a piece of pastry in each mold and trim the edges.

4. Pierce the bottom of the pastry base with a fork and then fill the molds with the topping.

5. Break up the cheese by hand and add a generous spoonful of goats' cheese to each tart. Cut the artichoke hearts into thin slices and place these on top of the tarts. Sprinkle each tart with chopped fresh chives and a pinch of black pepper.

6. Put the tarts in the oven - preheated to 225°C - for about 10 minutes. Then reduce the temperature to 200°C until the cream is curdled and the pastry begins to brown.

7. Remove the tarts from the oven. Serve them hot or cold, garnished with some fresh, chopped chives.

---o0o---

2.16 Cheese tapas

Spain has a vast number of excellent cheeses, including 23 cheeses that are protected under the Denominación de Origen (D.O.) system of Spain and the European Union.

The country has a large production of goats', sheep and cows' milk and produces many cheeses made with each of these, but also many cheeses made with milk blended from all of these. Spain still produces various cheeses made from raw (un-pasteurised) milk. Cheeses range in maturity and type from fresh cheese, through immature cheese (tierno), semi-mature cheese (semi-curado) and mature cheese (curado) to extra mature cheese (viejo).

As a very general rule, the stronger cheeses, such as Manchego, tend to be sheep milk cheese, whilst goats' milk cheeses tend to be less strong. The lightest cheeses tend to be those made from cows' milk. However, there are many exceptions to these rules about taste. Spain also has a whole range of moulded cheeses, as well as smoked and herbal cheeses.

In many ways, Spain is very lucky to have held on to its handmade artisan cheese industry, and for the cheese connoisseur Spain is a paradise. In every region there is a wealth of local cheese varieties. Farmhouse cheese manufacture is still an important and traditional activity in every part of Spain and in some parts of the country every village has its own speciality.

Cheese is a popular ingredient in many tapas and many regional tapas take advantage of their local cheese products.

ALBÓNDIGAS DE QUESO

Cheese Fritters

These cheese balls are a simple and tasty tapa. You should choose a cheese that melts well and is easy to grate like a semi-mature (semi-curado) cheese of mixed cows', goats' and sheep milk. You can also use Manchego cheese if you want to have a very strong cheese taste. It grates and melts very well.

Ingredients:

> 300 g of grated cheese
> 2 eggs
> Flour
> Olive oil
> Salt to taste

Preparation:

1. Mix the grated cheese with the eggs, a little salt and a pinch of flour (about 5 g).

2. Blend the mixture together until the resulting dough can be formed into balls.

3. Coat the balls with flour and fry them in hot olive oil.

4. When browned, place them on kitchen paper to drain.

5. Serve hot with a tomato or alioli sauce.

BOLITAS DE QUESO DE CABRA FRESCO

Fresh Goats' Cheese and Garlic Canapé

Ingredients:

200 g of fresh goats' cheese
1 teaspoon of honey
Pepper
6 cloves of garlic
Paprika powder
Olive oil
Salt

Preparation:

1. Mix the cheese in a bowl with honey and a little pepper and salt (to your taste). Use a fork to blend the cheese until you have a paste.

2. Take small portions, and shape them into little balls.

3. Thinly slice the peeled garlic and fry it in a little olive oil until golden brown. When it is ready, take it from the heat and stir in the paprika powder. Pour this over the cheese balls.

4. Serve in small bowls with a piece of bread.

ENSALADA DE QUESO DE CABRA Y MERMELADA DE TOMATE

Goats' Cheese and Tomato Jam

Ingredients:

> Tomato jam (see recipe)
> Goats' cheese - "Rulo de Cabra" (1 slice per person)
> Assorted salad leaves
> Olive oil
> Salt
> Vinegar of Jerez

Preparation:

1. Place a layer of mixed salad leaves in a flat dish: rocket, cress, cos lettuce, lamb's lettuce, endive, etc. Sprinkle with salt.

2. Mix the olive oil and vinegar together and dress the leaves with this mixture.

3. Cut slices of goats' cheese in half. Place these on the top of the leaves and spoon a drop of tomato jam on each piece of cheese.

4. Serve as a tapa, accompanied by a small slice of bread.

ENSALADA DE TETILLA

Galician Tetilla Cheese Salad

This is a light salad made with tetilla cheese. Tetilla is the most characteristic cheese from Galicia, and since 1993 is one of four cheeses made in Galicia with a European certified denomination of origin. The cheese was originally produced in the small towns along the border between the provinces of A Coruña and Pontevedra, such as Arzúa, Melide, Curtis or Sobrado dos Monxes, but the cheese is now produced in the whole of Galicia. The milk used comes mainly from the Galician Blond cow breed. The name tetilla (Spanish for breast) describes the shape of the cheese, a sort of cone.

Ingredients:

> 1 lettuce, washed, dried and shredded (or mixed salad leaves)
> 60 ml of olive oil
> 20 ml of sherry vinegar
> Garlic, to taste, crushed
> Salt
> Pepper
> 200 g of tetilla cheese, cut into small cubes
> 100 g of black or green olives, stoned
> 100 g of tomatoes (chopped roughly)

Preparation:

1. Put the lettuce, or leaves, into a serving dish with some chopped tomatoes.

2. Make a dressing with the oil, the vinegar and seasoning, and pour this over the lettuce and tomato. Mix thoroughly.

3. Mix the cubes of tetilla with the olives and add them to the leaves.

4. Serve immediately in small individual bowls with a slice of bread.

ENVUELTOS DE BERENJENA CON QUESO DE BURGOS

Aubergine Rolls with Burgos Cheese

This tapa is made using "requesón", which is a soft, white whey cheese, similar to ricotta in consistency, though not as sweet. It is a traditional cheese of Spain and Portugal, used for spreads and generally available in any Spanish grocery shop - but ricotta can be used if you can't find authentic requesón.

Requesón is manufactured in the regions of Cantabria, Galicia and the Pyrenees but the most famous variant of this cheese is "Queso de Burgos" which is made with sheep milk and is still sold by the farmers/producers at the weekly market in Burgos.

Ingredients:

>3 aubergines
>5-6 tablespoons of olive oil
>3 large cloves of garlic
>250 ml of fresh cheese, such as requesón or "queso de Burgos"
>1 large red pepper
>150 ml of sun-dried tomatoes in oil

Sauce:

>Serve with either mojo verde, mojo picón (see recipes under "Sauces") or just a plain homemade tomato sauce, according to taste.

Preparation:

1. Wash the aubergines and discard the stems. Cut the aubergines lengthwise into slices of about 1 cm thick. Brush these with olive oil and grill them on both sides until soft. Remove them from the grill and leave to cool.

2. Peel and slice the garlic. Heat it gently in some olive oil until the garlic is warm, but not browned. Remove from the heat but leave the garlic in the oil for 5-10 minutes. When cool, mix the oil and garlic with the requesón cheese in a mixing bowl. Set aside.

3. Prepare the sauce of your choice (see the recipes under "Sauces" in this book).

4. Roast a red pepper in the oven until it begins to blacken at the edges. Remove the seeds and stem and cut the roasted red pepper into strips. Drain the sun-dried tomatoes and cut them into strips.

5. Slice up a baguette or similar bread. Toast the slices lightly on both sides and add a few drops of olive oil.

6. Spread the cheese on a slice of the aubergine and put 2-3 sun-dried tomato strips on top. Add a piece of roasted red pepper and more cheese. Then, roll up the aubergine slice with its filling and place the rolls carefully in an ovenproof dish. Grill the rolls until the aubergine begins to brown slightly (just 1 or 2 minutes). Take them from the grill and cover with mojo or tomato sauce.

7. Serve each aubergine roll hot on a small plate on top of a slice of toasted baguette and plenty of sauce.

PALITOS CRUJIENTES DE QUESO Y MEMBRILLO
Crunchy Cheese Sticks and Quince

Torta del Casar is a cheese made from sheep milk in the Extremadura region. It is named after Casar de Cáceres, its city of origin. The milk is curdled using a coagulant found in the cardoon, a wild thistle. This ingredient gives a slight bitterness to this rich and slightly salty cheese. The cheese is aged for at least sixty days. The fully ripe cheese has a creamy consistency in the centre, and is traditionally eaten by slicing off the top and scooping out the inside. The cheese has the protected-origin status and can only be made with the milk of Merino and Entrefina sheep.

This recipe is an example of using the sweet membrillo jelly (quince jelly) in combination with a rich cheese flavour.

Ingredients:

> Sheets of filo pastry
> Torta del Casar cheese
> Quince jelly
> Olive oil
> 1 egg yolk

Preparation:

1. Preheat the oven to 200°C. Cool the cheese down in the deep freeze to make it more workable.

2. Carefully separate some sheets of filo pastry, lay them out and baste them with some olive oil. Put a second sheet on top of the oiled ones, spread some more oil on the top and cut them into triangles with a sharp knife. Spoon a portion of Torta del Casar cheese in the wide area of each triangle. Roll the pastry up towards the top of the triangle. Gently close the ends of the sticks so that no cheese leaks out when they are baked in the oven.

3. Paint the sticks with egg yolk and bake them for about 5-7 minutes until golden and they have become crisp and brittle.

4. Cut the quince jelly into square or rectangular pieces and place one of these on top of each cheese stick. Serve immediately.

PINCHO DE QUESO SAN SIMÓN Y AGUACATE

Cheese San Simón with Avocado

San Simón cheese is a smoked cheese made in Galicia from cows' milk. It is a cheese with D.O. protection, originally produced in mediaeval times in the Sierras de A Carba and O Xistral. It is matured for a minimum of 30 days and after maturing is smoked, always using birch bark. The cheese has a characteristic pear shape and is semi-hard with a creamy texture. It has a mild flavour, with hints of a spicy, smoky aroma.

Here it combines very well with avocado in a delicious, simple tapa.

Ingredients:

>4 slices of country bread
>4 slices of San Simón da Costa cheese
>A mix of fresh, young salad leaves (lettuce, spinach, chard, etc.)
>1 ripe avocado
>1 tablespoon of lemon juice
>Half a teaspoon of dried chilli (to taste)
>Freshly ground black pepper
>Salt

Preparation:

1. Wash and dry the salad leaves.

2. Toast the slices of bread.

3. Peel the avocado, take out the stone and put the flesh in a bowl. Add the lemon juice, chilli, black pepper and a pinch of salt. Mash with a fork to make it into a smooth paste.

4. Just before serving spread the avocado mixture on the slices of toasted bread. Place the young leaves on top of the avocado spread.

5. Partly melt the slices of cheese in a grill for a very short time, place them on top of the leaves. Put the pinchos under the grill for a few seconds before serving.

6. Garnish with a slice of tomato or with a cherry tomato.

PROVOLONE AL HORNO CON TOMATE Y ORÉGANO

Provolone Cheese Baked with Tomato and Oregano

Despite the fact that provolone is an Italian cheese, we included this tapa recipe simply because it is so popular. Also, the close political and culinary links between Spain and Southern Italy from the 13th century until the 19th century mean that many similar cheeses exist in both countries. Indeed, it is quite likely that the humble pizza was developed during the Spanish rule of Naples. Thus you can easily substitute provolone with one of the many similar cheeses which have been made in both countries for centuries. For example, you can use the famous "queso de servilleta" of Cataluña, which behaves in a similar way to provolone when baked and grilled.

Ingredients:

> 1 clove of garlic
> 2 medium-sized tomatoes
> 1 piece of provolone cheese (about 250 grams)
> Oregano to taste
> Thyme
> Salt to taste
> Black pepper to taste

Preparation:

1. Peel the garlic clove and rub an earthenware casserole with it so it absorbs the taste.

2. Cut one tomato into slices and the other one into cubes.

3. Season the tomato with salt and pepper and arrange the slices in the bottom of the casserole. Sprinkle them with oregano. Place the provolone cheese on top of the tomato slices and finish off with putting the diced tomato around the edges and on top of the cheese. Add a little more oregano.

4. Put the casserole in a pre-heated oven at 200°C just above the middle of the oven until the cheese is browned. This can take up to 25 minutes but keep an eye on it. Finish off under the grill for 5 minutes.

5. When the cheese is melted and golden, serve the dish at once, sprinkled with thyme, with some fresh country bread or slices of toast.

QUESO ASADO DE LA PALMA CON MOJO

Grilled Cheese of La Palma with Mojo

Grilled cheese with mojo is a typical dish from the Islas Canarias, specifically from the island of La Palma. The most traditional recipe uses the smoked Palmero cheese, but any other smoked goats' cheese can be used.

The Palmero cheese is made with un-pasteurised goats' milk and has protection of the Denomination of Origin (D.O.). The cheese is made on many small farms all over the island. Some of the cheese is sold as it is and some is smoked in the traditional way over open fires. The flavour is clean and characteristic of goats' cheese and has a very slight smoky taste.

Ingredients:

> 1 kg of smoked goats' cheese (Palmero)
> 200 ml. of green mojo (see recipes under "Sauces")

Preparation:

1. Cut the cheese into slices, each with a thickness of about 1 cm. Don't remove the cheese rind because this is where most of the smoky flavour is concentrated.

2. Put a few drops of olive oil on a griddle or in a non-stick frying pan and spread the oil. Heat it.

3. When the oil is very hot put the cheese slices in the pan or on the griddle. Allow the cheese to brown a little on both sides but do not let it melt.

4. Take it off the heat as soon as it has browned slightly. Place a slice on individual plates, pour some green mojo on top and serve immediately.

QUESO DE CABRA EN ACEITE

Goats' Cheese in Olive Oil

Marinating cheese in olive oil is a way of preserving fresh cheese for a few extra weeks, whilst infusing it with the taste of herbs and spices.

In this tapa, young or semi-matured (semi-curado) goats' cheese is preserved in olive oil with herbs and spices, stored in the refrigerator so that the flavours of the garlic, thyme and rosemary become infused into the oil. Note that it is important to ensure that you treat the herbs and spices with lemon juice (or vinegar) before adding the olive oil and to make sure the mix is stored in the refrigerator. Also select an olive oil that you like. It shouldn't be too overwhelming or the oil will mask the taste of the cheese and herbs.

A similar recipe can also be used for sheep cheese and for more mature cheeses, although generally, mature cheeses or the stronger sheep cheeses are eaten as they are. If you choose to marinate them in oil, these harder cheeses are usually cut into long sticks of 1 to 2 cm thickness before placing them vertically in the oil.

Ingredients:

> 350 g young or semi-mature goats' cheese
> 1 teaspoon of dried thyme (or 2 sprigs of fresh thyme)
> 1 teaspoon of dried rosemary (or 2 small sprigs of fresh rosemary)
> 4 large cloves of garlic
> Half a teaspoon of black, red and white peppercorns
> 1 or 2 small chilli peppers
> Olive oil
> Juice of half a lemon or equivalent in white wine vinegar

Preparation:

1. Sterilise a preserving jar by washing it and then putting it into an oven pre-heated to 150°C for 5-10 minutes.

2. Peel the garlic cloves and crush them. Place the garlic, thyme, rosemary and pepper into the dry, sterilised preserving jar. Add a generous squeeze of lemon juice to the herbs and spices and make sure that they are all thoroughly coated. Leave this mixture to stand for an hour.

3. Half fill the preserving jar with olive oil.

4. Cut the cheese into 2 cm cubes and place them into jar. Top up the jar with olive oil, close it and place it in the refrigerator. This can be stored for up to 1 week in the refrigerator, but not longer.

5. Allow the cheese to marinate for at least 24 hours.

6. Serve the cheese with slices of baguette and the infused oil.

QUESO DE CABRA REBOZADO
Breaded Goats' Cheese

Ingredients:

Beer
Chickpea flour
Breadcrumbs
Goats' cheese (Rulo de Cabra)
Olive oil
Homemade tomato sauce
Almonds

Preparation:

1. Mix the beer and flour together until obtaining a batter with the texture of beaten egg.

2. Cut the cheese into slices with a thickness of about 1-2 cm.

3. Dip the slices of cheese in the beer mix and then coat them with the breadcrumbs, then again in the batter and again in the breadcrumbs, forming a thick coating of crumbs.

4. Fry the breaded cheese in hot olive oil and serve hot with a light tomato sauce and a sprinkling of finely chopped almonds.

QUESO MANCHEGO Y DULCE DE MEMBRILLO

Manchego Cheese and Quince Jelly

Quince jelly, also known as dulce de membrillo, is a sweet, thick jelly made of the pulp of the quince fruit and has been made since Roman times. It is often served in Spain as an accompaniment to cheese. The sweetness of the quince jelly contrasts well with a strong cheese, such as one of the matured cheeses of La Mancha.

Manchego cheese is probably the most famous Spanish cheese and has its own Denomination of Origin. According to the regulations of the denomination, the cheese must be made from the milk of Manchego sheep of the Entrefino breed. It is a strong and buttery cheese and is soft and crumbly in texture. It is aged for between 60 days and 2 years.

Ingredients:

> 200 g Manchego cheese
> 150 g quince jelly (in a block)

Preparation:

1. Cut the cheese into wedges of about 5mm thick.

2. Cut slices or small blocks of quince jelly. Place a piece with each slice of cheese.

3. Serve the cheese and quince jelly alone on a small plate or with some bread.

REMOLACHAS CON QUESO DE CABRA A LA PLANCHA

Marinated Beetroot with Grilled Goats' Cheese

This recipe uses a type of fresh goats' cheese which normally comes in a roll with a white mold skin. There are several of these cheeses, especially in the País Vasco (Bettine, for instance). They grill quite well and have a strong taste. They are known in Spain as "rulo de queso de cabra". This recipe uses a base of beetroot salad but this grilled cheese can be successfully served with any kind of salad and many different sauces as we can see in other recipes in this book.

Ingredients:

> Olive oil
> Red wine vinegar
> 1 teaspoon of sugar
> 1 teaspoon of thyme leaves
> 4 raw beetroot, peeled and very thinly sliced
> Salt and pepper
> 2 x 100 g young goats' cheese rounds with rind, in slices of 1cm thick
> 4 handfuls of rocket or other salad leaf

Preparation:

1. Make a marinade by mixing some olive oil, vinegar, sugar and thyme in a shallow dish and season well with salt and pepper. Add the sliced beetroot and marinate for at least 1 hour or, better still, overnight.

2. Heat the grill to a high temperature. Season the goats' cheese slices with a little salt and pepper, then place them on an oiled baking tray and grill them for 2-3 min. until golden and melting.

3. Put the slices of beetroot on individual small plates and top with a piece of goats' cheese. Add some of the salad leaves and finish off by pouring some of the marinade over the salad and cheese.

RULO DE CABRA A LA PLANCHA CON MERMELADA DE TOMATE

Grilled Goats' Cheese with Tomato Jam

This is a classic cheese tapa found in many variations throughout Spain. The goats' cheese is quite strong and, when grilled, makes a perfect combination with the sweet tomato jam.

Ingredients:

>   Large round slices of goats' cheese (1-2 cm thick)
>   Olive oil
>   Tomato jam at room temperature (see recipe in "Sauces")

Preparation:

1. Put a drop of olive oil in a frying pan. Fry the cheese on high heat on both sides for 1-2 minutes each side. It should be toasted rather than melted.

2. Serve in a bowl with a tablespoon of tomato jam on top, with an optional slice of crusty bread.

TOSTADO DE PAN GALLEGO CON QUESO ARZÚA Y MIEL

Toasted Galician Bread with Arzúa Cheese and Honey

Cheese and honey is another very Spanish combination of savoury and sweet flavours, found here in a Galician tapa recipe from Ourense.

This simple tapa is made with Galician bread, like Pan de Cea. This is white country bread with a light and crusty texture. The cheese used is Queso Arzúa which is a cows' milk cheese of the D.O. Arzúa-Ulloa. Queso Arzúa is a soft cheese, made from raw or pasteurized milk with a short maturity period. It is creamy with a slightly sweet flavour similar to the other famous Galician cheese "Tetilla"

Ingredients:

> 200 g of Arzúa Cheese
> 6 slices of Galician bread Pan de Cea
> 2 tablespoons of honey

Preparation:

1. Slice the bread and toast it lightly on both sides.

2. Cut the cheese into slices and place one on each slice of bread.

3. Spoon a little honey on top of the cheese.

3. Place the bread under a grill for a few minutes until the cheese begins to melt slightly.

4. Serve warm on a small plate.

---oOo---

2.17 Sweet tapas

Sweet tapas are not as common as savoury tapas, but they do exist and are quite popular during the summer months when there is an abundance of fruit on the market in Spain. The mixture of sweet and savoury tastes has a long tradition in Spain, stretching back to Moorish times.

CARNE DE MEMBRILLO Y MANZANAS
Quince and Apple Jelly

This is a tasty and sweet conserve, which can be stored for a long time and is excellent as an accompaniment to cheeses, dried fruits, and nuts or together with fruit tarts. It's often used as part of a tapa.

Ingredients:

> 1 kg of quinces (membrillo)
> 700 g of cooking apples
> 1 medium-sized peeled lemon (without the pith)
> 1.5 kg of sugar
> Cinnamon stick

Preparation:

1. Wash the quinces well, to remove the "fluff" on the outside of the fruit. Put the fruits whole into a pan with plenty of water and simmer for about 40 minutes together with a whole cinnamon stick.

2. Let the pan cool and carefully remove the skin, core and seeds from the quinces.

3. Peel and core the apples. Weigh the total amount of fruit and then add the same weight in sugar. Add the finely-chopped lemon and leave all to simmer in the pan over a medium heat, without boiling, stirring frequently and being careful to avoid burning.

4. Gradually the mix changes colour and consistency as it becomes darker and thicker. The cooking time will vary, depending on the amount of pectin in the fruit.

5. When the mix has the consistency of a thick jam, pour it into suitably shaped (long narrow) containers and let it cool completely. Serve it in slices.

CARNE DE MEMBRILLO (II)

Quince Jelly (II)

Quince jelly is traditionally served with cheese and makes a delightful combination with a piece of strong Manchego cheese.

Ingredients:

> Quince
> Sugar - use about the same weight of sugar as there is quince after it is boiled and cleaned
> Cinnamon
> Cloves (to taste)

Preparation:

1. Wash the quinces and boil them in a saucepan with water until they are tender.

2. Leave them to cool, then peel them and remove the cores.

3. Blend the quince in a blender, add sugar and cinnamon and then blend again.

4. Bring the blended mix to the boil (with the cloves), stirring constantly until it reaches the desired consistency (something like a thick jam).

5. Remove the cloves. Pour the hot mixture into long, narrow, deep containers and allow it to cool and set.

6. Serve the jelly cut into slices.

CEBOLLA CARAMELIZADA

Caramelized Onion

Caramelised onion is simple to make and can be used with many other tapa dishes. For example, goats' cheese ("rulo de cabra") on toast with caramelised onion is a delicious contrast of savoury and sweet tastes.

Ingredients:

> 3 large onions
> 50 g of brown sugar
> 500 ml of Pedro Ximenez sweet wine, or brandy
> Olive oil
> Vinegar of Jerez (to taste)

Preparation

1. Cut the onions into thin strips and fry them in a little olive oil until golden brown.

2. Add the brandy or wine and let the alcohol evaporate.

3. Finally, stir in the brown sugar and keep stirring until it caramelizes. Add vinegar to taste.

4. Serve.

HOJALDRE CON BREVAS, QUESO Y AVELLANAS

Figs, Cheese and Hazelnuts on Puff Pastry

When there is a fig harvest, there is often a very large one. Fig trees are prolific producers of fruit and a single tree is more than enough for a family. There are several types of fig which are distinguished by size and colour. In this case the recipe uses the "brevas", which are the first crop in late spring and early summer, but any other fresh fig may be used.

Ingredients:

> Fresh puff pastry
> 4 figs
> 50 g of cottage cheese ("requesón")
> 25 g of goats' cheese ("rulo de cabra")
> 25 g of Manchego cheese
> Black pepper
> 30 grams of milk
> A few leaves of lettuce or other salad leaf
> 8 hazelnuts

Honey Vinaigrette

> 3 tablespoons of olive oil
> Half a tablespoon of sherry vinegar
> 1 tablespoon of honey
> A pinch of salt

Preparation:

1. Prepare the pastry: spread it on a work surface and cut it into rectangles a bit wider than the slices of fig. Place them in an oven tray on baking paper. Cover with another sheet of baking paper and an oven tray on top of this to stop the pastry puffing up too much when baking.

2. Bake the pastry in a preheated oven at 200°C for about 20 minutes. When it is browned, place the pastry on a rack to cool.

3. Mix the chopped goats' cheese (rulo de cabra) with the cottage cheese (requesón) and the freshly grated manchego cheese in a blender. Stir in milk and some freshly ground black pepper. Blend until the mixture has a smooth, creamy, spreadable texture.

4. Wash and dry some lettuce leaves, wash the figs and cut them into slices. Chop the hazelnuts finely.

5. Prepare the vinaigrette by mixing all the ingredients and whisking vigorously.

6. Just before serving the tapa, spread the pastry with the cheese, put some lettuce leaves on top and then the slices of fig and the chopped hazelnuts. Finally pour over a little of the vinaigrette.

SALMOREJO DE MANGO
Mango Gazpacho

The months of July and August are torrid in most of Spain and this is the time for all kinds of cold soups. It is the season of gazpachos. Here is one which combines both traditional savoury ingredients with sweet mango.

Ingredients:

> 1 kg of ripe tomatoes
> 1-2 cloves of garlic
> 1 teaspoon of salt
> 30 ml of vinegar
> 100 ml of olive oil
> Half a mango, peeled

Preparation:

1. Put all the ingredients in a blender and blend until it has the consistency of a thick soup.

2. Place the gazpacho in the fridge and serve chilled with chopped hard-boiled egg (optionally).

SORBETE DE APIO Y LIMON

Celery and Lemon Sorbet

Ingredients:

> 150 g of sugar
> The juice of 4 lemons
> 350 g of celery stalks with leaves
> 1 litre of water
> Celery leaves for garnish

Preparation:

1. Blend the lemon juice and celery together in the blender. Pass the mixture through a sieve.

2. Mix the juice together with 750 ml of water and the sugar. Mix well and blend again for a few seconds.

3. Put the mixture in the freezer for at least 5 hours, stirring at intervals of about 1 hour to get it to freeze but without producing a frozen block. When ice crystals have started to form it is ready to serve.

4. If you prepare the sorbet in advance, keep stirring the mix every hour to keep the correct consistency.

5. Serve in glasses and garnish with a celery leaf.

---oOo---

List of Recipes - Spanish Names

---oOo---

List of Recipes - English Names

---o0o---

About the Author

Malcolm Coxall, the author, is the proprietor of the family's 110 acre organic farm in Southern Andalucía in Spain. The farm produces olives, almonds and culinary herbs. It incorporates a small factory for the packing of organic herbs, dried fruits and nuts.

Apart from running the farm, Malcolm also provides IT consultancy and business services especially to other organic food producers in the region. He has published several books and many articles on traditional Spanish food, sustainable agriculture, organic food production, forest biodiversity, environmental protection, politics and economics. He is active in the European food and environmental movement, and has taken several successful legal actions in defence of European environmental standards in the European Court of Justice.

Malcolm is passionate about local food production, culinary diversity, agricultural sustainability and traditional gastronomy. He believes that our traditional recipes have much to teach a generation that lives on a largely homogenised processed diet and has basically forgotten how real food is grown and prepared. He believes that truly *good* food is local, ethical, organic and slow and that how and what we eat defines who we are as a society. Malcolm is a lifelong vegetarian but also loves good food and sees no dichotomy between the two.

As he says: "Societies that knowingly eat chemically adulterated junk foods, produced in heartless factory farms, reveal an intrinsic social, political and health malaise and a profound lack of empathy for the planet. How can such food be *good* food? It cannot. Such societies reveal their lack of sustainability, an inherent ignorance of the world we share and a disconnection from their natural and social context. Contrast this "care-less" mentality with those societies which treasure their land, their natural environment, their people, their traditional cuisine and the quality of their food.

"Spanish traditional food is one of the last bastions of good food in Europe. The Spanish are fiercely proud of their local agricultural produce and with some justification. Few other culinary traditions in Europe are as vast in range, as imaginative, healthy and delicious as that of Spain. The Spanish love good food and good company, they enjoy life and they love their land and its produce. Tapas are a source of great pride throughout the country and, despite many preconceptions, are a great alternative for the vegetarian.

"Asking for a vegetarian dish in a Spanish restaurant will rarely raise an eyebrow and you can be sure that the chef will do anything to oblige you. This imaginative and caring attitude is a breath of fresh air in a world of fast, cheap and cheerful fodder for the masses.

"Explain to me again why we need fast food and how 'industrial agriculture' fits in with the larger concepts of human and environmental well-being and sustainability. To be sustainable, we need to start to understand food again - beginning with the basics - both on the farm and in the kitchen. To begin, we could do worse than to try to re-discover our own local gastronomic heritage. Not only is this socially worthwhile and important, it is also great fun to discover how to make and enjoy real food again."

Malcolm Coxall

Málaga 2014

---oOo---

Printed in Great Britain
by Amazon.co.uk, Ltd.,
Marston Gate.